Praise for
The Day You Love Me

"Humphrey's collection offers **confident and assured storytelling with unforgettable characters that stay with the reader long after the last page is turned** ... Humphrey is especially adept at examining the hidden lives of his characters and the secrets that drive their actions...It is fitting that most of the stories are set overseas, as love is foreign territory for the protagonists. The settings, which range from Japan to France, are well-drawn and complement the developing bonds. **Accomplished and consistently engaging tales of romance**."

—*Kirkus Reviews*

"This luscious collection is a sensual passport to discovery. Jay Lewis Humphrey gives readers **a fiercely original voice** in this debut collection of short stories. Snuggle in for a great read!"

—Sharon O. Lightholder, author
The English Rendition and
The Baldwin Portolano

"*The Day You love Me* is an **intimate adventure of travel, life and love** shared in a witty, wonderful way."

—Sally Kuhlman
Sally Around the Bay

"*The Day You Love Me* is a collection of six **deliciously inventive love stories**, rollercoastering the reader through suspense, sensuality, and secrets; desire, despair, and danger. (As one of the characters says, "The worst they can do is kill me. Hopefully, not until morning.") Best of all, **Humphrey knows how to twist a tale with humor, surprise, and very sweet revenge.**"

—Laurie McAndish King, author
Lost, Kidnapped, Eaten Alive! and
Your Crocodile Has Arrived

"*The Day You Love Me* is a **skillfully written collection of engaging stories about memorable characters.** A satisfying read."

—Susan Bays, publisher
Arbutus Press

"All you need is love, sang the Beatles. Yes, sure, but love, whatever that is, is easier to sing about than to attain … or keep. Jay Lewis Humphrey, in his delightfully quirky collection of stories, gives us six deftly crafted variations on this eternal theme. Whether the tale takes place in the heart of Paris or near the foot of Mt. Fuji, **you, the reader, are there—caring, contemplating, chuckling, always fully engaged.**"

—Philip O. Chomak, author
Beside the Point: Close Encounters in the Global Classroom

"**The illustration style is a bold and refreshing visual choice**, perfectly complementing these intriguing stories that follow some of the many paths that love might take."

—yAYu Tseng, artist, translator

"**The writing is so vivid,** I was immediately transported to each setting—and the emotions so real, **I was sometimes brought to tears.**"

—Deb Chandler, Norwich, England

THE
DAY
YOU
love
ME

THE DAY YOU *love* ME

Jay Lewis Humphrey

Keranen Press

Copyright © 2015, 2017 Jay Lewis Humphrey

All rights reserved. No part of this publication may be reproduced, distributed, or transmitted in any form or by any means, including photocopying, recording, or other electronic or mechanical methods, without the prior written permission of the publisher, except in the case of brief quotations embodied in critical reviews and certain other noncommercial uses permitted by copyright law.

This is a work of fiction. Names, characters, dialogues, businesses, places, events and incidents are either the products of the author's imagination or used in a fictitious manner. Any resemblance to actual persons, living or dead, is purely coincidental.

Published in the United States by Keranen Press
San Rafael, California

ISBN (print): 978-0-9981960-3-9
ISBN (eBook): 978-0-9981960-4-6

Publisher's Cataloging-in-Publication data

Names: Humphrey, Jay Lewis, author.
Title: The Day you love me / Jay Lewis Humphrey.
Description: San Rafael, CA: Keranen Press, 2017.
Identifiers: ISBN 978-0-9981960-3-9 (pbk.) |
978-0-9981960-4-6 (ebook)
Subjects: LCSH Man-Woman relationships—Fiction. | Love—Fiction. | Short stories, American. | BISAC FICTION / Short Stories (single author)
Classification:
LCC PS3608.U471 D39 2017 | DDC 813.6—dc23

Cover design and interior illustrations by Eliza Frye
(elizafrye.com)
Book design by Jim Shubin
(bookalchemist.net)

For Terry

Failure and success are equally dangerous.
    —LAO-TZU

CONTENTS

- 1   KEIKO
- 37   PING—CLICK
- 85   FLY GIRL
- 151   FREEDOM
- 169   MEN AND DOGS
- 209   THE DAY YOU LOVE ME

KEIKO

"I AM CAT," KEIKO WHISPERS AS SHE SLOWLY RUNS her fingers along my chest beneath my frayed, light-cotton shirt. We're lying together at twilight on reed mats beside a rice paddy near Mt. Fuji. Of course I desperately want to kiss her, to make love to her, but I'm on high alert. I've known Keiko for less than 48 hours, and post-war Japan is a mystery to me. The last thing I want to do is break any cultural taboos and find myself skewered on a razor-sharp sword.

My name's Jari—pronounced "Yari"—Keranen. I'm 19 years old, and though I was born in Helsinki, my parents emigrated from Finland to the States when I was a child. So now, I guess, I'm officially a Finnish-American. A couple days ago, I left my new friend Bill in our cheap hotel in Tokyo to take a four- or five-day walk in the Japanese countryside. Bill, an ex-Marine, strongly advised me not to do this. "If you insist on strolling alone in the boondocks," he said, "be very careful, especially of the men. They have no reason to like us. And they don't. Besides, you know there's a typhoon on its way." I decided to take my "stroll" anyway.

I took an afternoon train out of the Tokyo sprawl, and arrived at sundown in a small town near Fuji, 24 hours before the typhoon hit. At the first tavern I saw, I decided I could afford a beer. As I was ordering my drink, two young women in kimonos approached and sat down next to me.

"Hi. I Keiko, she Michiko."

My eyes widen as I look at the speaker. Dark almond eyes, delicate nose, her face a cool, Asian Modigliani. "Hello." I'm not real good at small talk. Just like my dad, though he swears he's not really taciturn. On the rare occasions that he speaks.

"You soldier?"

"No." Time to try out a Japanese phrase Bill taught me. "*Watashi-wa bimbo-na daigakusei desu*—I'm a poor university student."

Her eyes narrow slightly. "You speak Japanese?"

"Only a few words. But where did you learn English?"

"Soldiers teach me." She tilts her head. "Why you here?"

I try to explain that I've been working and traveling for a year on a very tight budget before going back to the comfortable confines of college.

She gives me a blank look. "Why you come this town?"

"My friend Bill in Tokyo said it was a beautiful place to hike. Good view of Fuji-san."

Abruptly, Michiko stands and smiles. She bows politely to me, walks to the other end of the bar and sits down next to a Japanese guy who's just come in.

Keiko continues to stare at me. "What your name?"

"Jari."

Her gaze never wavers. "How long you stay here?"

"Maybe three or four more days. Then I go back to Tokyo."

She considers this information for a moment. "Why you come Japan?"

"I'm trying to understand more, see new things."

"Where you live?"

"Cedar Grove, a small town surrounded by farms in a state with many cows."

"What cows?"

"Animals. Big animals." No response. "You know—

milk, cheese, these are made from cows. They have black and white spots, eat grass, and have big eyes." Jesus! How do you describe a cow to someone who speaks a different language and may never have seen one? I know the Japanese have milk, but so far I haven't seen a cow in Tokyo, Yokohama, or the countryside. And why am I trying to describe a cow to this beautiful woman? Dead end. Change the subject. "You live here in town?"

She nods her head. "Yes."

"Are you a student, too?"

Keiko frowns. "No. I work sometimes in bar."

Okay, a bar hostess. I feel very sophisticated knowing that bars sometimes pay women to get male customers to buy them drinks. So what should I do now? Buy her a drink? If she orders champagne, there goes my week's budget. Besides, I don't want to *pay* her to talk to me, to be just another customer that she entertains to make a few dollars. But I have to ask her. "You want me to buy you a drink?"

She glances quickly at the woman bartender serving drinks to Michiko and her new acquaintance. "No," Keiko whispers, and stands up. "You go now. Come back midnight. Here, meet me."

For a moment, I wonder if this is really happening.

She won't let me buy her a drink, and she wants to meet me at midnight? "Okay. Yes. Here, in the bar?"

"No, outside."

"Sure. Midnight. Twelve o'clock. Outside."

"Yes."

"Good. Wonderful. See you then. Midnight. Outside."

"Yes."

I decide to try out the second Japanese phrase that Bill armed me with. "*Anata-wa utsukushii desu*—You are beautiful."

Keiko smiles. "We take bath," she says, and then walks over to join Michiko.

Take a bath? Together? At least Keiko doesn't seem to hate me. I finish my beer in one gulp, look at my watch, nod to the woman behind the bar, pick up my backpack and leave.

As I drift about the quiet town, I ponder my situation. After working in Honolulu, I've been traveling alone in Asia, taking passage on rusty tramp steamers and ferries, wandering from Manila up through Macao and Hong Kong to Yokohama and Tokyo. On land, I eat street food, sleep in dismal hotels, and occasionally find refuge on the floor of a kindly missionary's hut. People on the street often stare at me like I'm some kind of pale, skinny scarecrow with blond hair and round, blue eyes. And I admit, armed only with my good intentions and shielded solely by my ignorance, I do sometimes feel very vulnerable.

I figure I know what Bill was warning me about. Though the atom bomb ended the conflict with Japan over a decade ago, World War II is still recent news in this region. And I grew up in an atmosphere of wartime fear and hatred, a world filled with enemies. When we left Finland for the U.S. in the summer of 1945, World War II in Europe was over, but the war with Japan was still going on. Everyone in the States was talking about the Japanese army's horrendous cruelty to millions of people. In America, Japan was the stuff of everyone's worst nightmares. Bill said that long before the war, the Japanese military was teaching the people to hate all foreigners. Even today, every *gaijin*—foreigner—is still a potential target.

Bill also told me about the harsh warrior code of *Bushido*—to die a noble death with one's personal honor intact is the ultimate goal of life. Keiko's father was probably a Japanese soldier. I'd better be very careful. Best to avoid all contact with her family, *especially* her father. Bill's warning rattled me more than I like to admit.

Just for luck, I touch my traveler's charm, my tiger

tooth that I wear on a slender gold-colored chain around my neck. I bought it in Hawaii. It's only a small piece of plastic shaped like a saber-toothed tiger's fang. I'm not superstitious enough to believe that it actually brings me good luck, but I treasure the necklace as a symbol of my time in Hawaii. I worked a variety of jobs: busboy, waiter, construction worker, parking lot attendant. During that time, I began to shed a portion of my college-boy insularity. My tiger tooth was a symbol of my graduation from books to the far less tidy realm of reality.

But all my historical musings evaporate when I imagine returning with Keiko to her apartment after the bath. I wander through the darkened lanes and alleys, impatient to see her again. This place sure seems to be deserted at night compared to the busy streets of Tokyo.

I still have hours to wait. I can't read Japanese, so I don't know the name of the bar nor do I know the streets of the town. But I'm secure in my well-honed sense of direction.

At last, it's almost midnight. Confidently, I walk to the bar, but it isn't there. The street seems familiar—perhaps the bar is one street over? A short walk. No. It isn't. I'm lost. I search desperately for over an hour, but everything is closed, dark and unfamiliar. Finally, I walk back to the railroad station at the foot of a dirt road that winds down a hill at the edge of town. The station is closed. Miserable, I lie down outside on a hard wooden bench beneath the overhanging roof, thinking that Keiko will believe I deliberately stood her up.

Early morning. I meander through the town till I find a tiny market open. After trading two small coins for a wizened orange, I set out to carefully explore each street. Hours later, a miracle! I think I've finally located the bar. It's a low, one-story wooden building with a dark gray, slanted roof and four yellow rice-paper windows crosshatched with split bamboo braces. Two small, cement garden-sculpture temples stand in front, one on each side of the shoji screen entrance. A red paper lantern hangs from the roof above each tiny statue. I take careful note of the nearby buildings, and then walk around the rest of the day, waiting for evening. I hope Keiko is working tonight.

At twilight, I return. The red lanterns are lit, and the door is open. I enter the bar, but I don't see Keiko. However, Michiko sees me. She comes over and looks at me suspiciously.

"Where you last night?"

"I couldn't help it, I got lost. The town, the darkness

confused me." Michiko gazes at me with polite disdain. "I'm telling you the truth. I looked for hours. I couldn't find the bar."

Her icy gaze softens fractionally. "Keiko wait for you."

"I'm sorry. I really want to see her. I want to very much. Please understand." But I don't think Michiko buys my story.

She gives me a dismissive frown. "Wait here. Keiko be here soon." A slight bow and she's gone. I sit down at the bar, order a beer, and glumly wait.

A half hour later, Keiko arrives, beautiful in her delicate kimono. She sees me. Absolutely no response. Michiko goes over to her and whispers a few words. Keiko looks at me, and then slowly walks over.

"Where you go last night?"

Again, I try to explain, angry with myself for not studying Japanese, for having the hubris to wander through this country expecting everyone to speak my language. "Please believe me, Keiko. I told Michiko, I got lost. I couldn't find the bar." Keiko gives a little sigh and looks away. "Please understand. I'm not lying. I want very much to see you." She doesn't speak. "Can we meet tonight? Please, I won't get lost again. I'll come back to the bar."

"No."

Is she punishing me? Or has she really lost all interest? One more try. "Keiko, honestly, I'm very sorry. Please meet me."

"Not at bar."

"Wonderful! I mean—okay. Where?"

"Where you stay last night?"

"The train station," I mutter.

She actually smiles. "Okay, train station."

"Yes! I'll meet you there at midnight. I promise."

"Yes," she says and walks back to Michiko.

The typhoon arrives in full force soon after I leave the bar. In five seconds, I'm drenched. The swirling wind pushes me one way, then another. I slog through the rain back to the station, push the long wooden bench into a corner, sit down at one end, my back against the wall, and pull my knees up to my chin. Better to huddle here than risk getting lost again in the storm. I have a long wait. The wind screams. The water seems to come from all directions in drops the size of tennis balls. The ditches alongside the dirt road are soon streams and then rushing rivers.

Finally, it's midnight. Stiff, wet and chilled in spite of the heat, I eagerly look for Keiko. When the lightning flashes, I see the road leading up the hill. Without the lightning, I see only a dim streetlight in front of the station. I wait—twelve twenty-five, twelve thirty. Where is she? Is she getting back at me? Didn't she believe me? Twelve forty-five. The lightning flashes again. In the distance, I see a tiny figure in a kimono weaving down the center of the muddy road. It's Keiko! It has to be. Buffeted by the shrieking wind and pummeled by the rain, I splash through the puddles up the road. Another lightning flash. A few more steps and she literally falls into my arms. Not from an excess of passion—from an excess of alcohol. She's staggering, falling-down drunk.

"Take me home," she mumbles, clinging to my neck with both arms.

I lift her up. She's remarkably light. "Tell me the way." She points toward the station. I carry her carefully back through the slippery mud down to my bench. "Now where?"

"There," she says, pointing to a narrow path that leads into the darkness away from the town.

But she said she lived in town. Is this some sort of trap? "Are you sure it's this way?"

"Go," she says. She lets her head roll back and opens her mouth to the pounding raindrops. Then she rolls it forward onto my shoulder again.

Outside the town, there are no streetlights, only the occasional flash of lightning. I walk for what seems like miles in the storm, following the muddy path on raised berms past innumerable rice paddies. Why does she live so far out of town? Suddenly, I'm scared. Where is she taking me? And why? But I can't just drop her in the mud. Guess I have to trust her. Anyway, I'm lost. Again.

At an intersection with another slippery mud levee, she points to the left. I turn and follow the new path. A lightning flash. Nearby, I see a small wood and paper house.

"There," she murmurs.

I set her down on a wooden step. She slides open a screen, reaches inside for a flashlight, and shines it on my muddy zoris. We remove our sandals and she leads me inside. I can make out several sleeping forms on the floor. I guess she has roommates.

She leads me to the left of the sleepers, and points to a mat a few feet away. "I sleep here tonight," she says. She quietly opens an interior screen and leads me into another room.

"Who are those people?" I whisper.

"Older brother, brother's wife, baby, mother, father," she whispers back.

"Your father?"

"Yes," she whispers, matter-of-factly.

Panic. What am I doing? An ignorant round-eye wandering into a nest of Samurai. What's her dad going to do if he finds a *gaijin* in his house in the morning? But where else can I go now? I haven't the faintest idea where I am. Oh, come on, Jari. Where's your *sisu*, that legendary Finnish fearlessness in the face of adversity? Perhaps that's a cultural trait that doesn't travel well, at least in my case. A blast of wind shakes the house and drives the rain sideways against the flimsy paper walls. Well, I'm certainly not going to spend the rest of the night wandering blindly in this storm. And Keiko doesn't seem worried, so trust her.

She takes my arm and begins to show me the room with her flashlight. In front of the screen opposite me, I see a dark porcelain basin, a large wooden tub, and a small table in the corner with a lantern on top. A few feet to my right, several reed mats hang from the ceiling. They partition off an area about four feet wide and six feet long. A good size for a coffin. She lifts up a hanging mat and points.

"That my bed. You sleep there." Her pillow is right next to the shoji screen that separates the tiny enclosure from her sleeping family.

She motions for me to remove my sodden clothes, gives me a small towel from the edge of the tub, points the flashlight at a blanket on her bed, then leaves me alone. In the darkness, I peel off my shirt and jeans, drape them over the edge of the tub, and dry myself with the towel. Then I carefully feel my way into the curtained-off area, lie down, and pull the blanket over me. Her family snores peacefully a few inches from my head. The rain pounds on the roof. The lightning flashes. I collapse into a dreamless sleep.

I wake up slowly, swimming to the surface of awareness, disoriented. The floor is hard, and the small cloth tube that functions as a pillow is harder. I feel adrift, not sure where I am. I open my eyes. Bright light from outside seeps through the shojis and the gaps in the hanging reed mats. It's completely silent. The typhoon has passed.

Where is everybody? I sit up, raise the reed curtain at my feet and crawl out of the tiny enclosure. The house seems empty. I struggle into my damp clothes and slide open the outer screen. The torrents of rain have given way to a flood of hot sunlight. Steam rises from the sodden earthen berms and the rice paddies, edged on all sides by tall grasses. A swamp smell hangs in the air. The sea of rice fields and the distant base of Fuji-san are a misty, shimmering, brilliant green. The sky is an intense blue, and the cone of Fuji a blinding white. It's so quiet that the sound of my own breathing seems an intrusion. I sit down on the wooden step and look at the mountain. The sun streams through the mist. I'm already sweating.

Eventually, the screen behind me opens softly. I twist around and see two women. The older woman must be Keiko's mother. But I'm confused when I look at the younger one. She looks very much like Keiko. Her brother's wife? Or *is* it Keiko, transformed into a different person away from the dim light of the bar and the brief flashes of lightning in the typhoon? I say nothing. Both women bow slightly and disappear back into the house. In a few moments, the older one reappears carrying a black lacquer tray with a small pot of tea, a cup, a pair of chopsticks and one fried egg on a tiny plate. Without looking directly at me, she kneels on the step, places the tray next to me, then quietly rises and departs. I wonder where the father and brother might be. And how they might feel today about having a *gaijin* sleeping in the house. But why should I be afraid now? They could have killed me in my sleep. Anyway, I'm innocent. All I did was carry Keiko home in a typhoon when she was drunk. And I wasn't the one who got her drunk. She could have fallen in a rice paddy and drowned. I brought her here safely. All I did was help, right?

Besides, I'm starving.

Clumsily, I divide the egg into quarters with the chopsticks. However, I discover that it's impossible for me to pick up a piece of greasy egg with them. I bring the plate up to my lips and push an egg fragment into my mouth. After savoring and swallowing each piece, I pour some tea into my cup. The egg was delicious, but even more delicious is the silent, hot mystery surrounding me. I sip the tea and continue to stare at the fields and the mountain.

I lose all track of time. An hour or perhaps two hours later, the screen again opens and Keiko sits down beside me. I know it's her this time. She presses next to me and puts her head against my shoulder.

She's so beautiful! I want to put my arm around her and pull her closer. But what would her family think? I'm not sure how I'd feel if my kid sister brought home some Japanese guy and told him to take her bed while she slept on the couch. But what if Keiko thinks I don't like her? Okay, this is her country; I'll follow her cues. She snuggles closer, puts her hand on my knee and squeezes it. I put my hand on her knee and gently squeeze back. She looks up at me, smiles, and softly kisses my neck.

But what now? Where can we go? Last night, I'd slept with my head about three inches from the rest of her family with only a thin screen separating us. It's out of the question that we could stay here together, even though she described the tiny chamber as her bedroom.

Suddenly Keiko stands up, motions for me to wait, and hurries into the house. She returns carrying two rolled up mats and a small paper box. Taking my hand, she leads me down the steps onto the raised dirt path. I follow her along the path across the vast expanse of neatly divided rice paddies and occasional clusters of other paper houses.

Long after her house is out of sight, we stop. She hands me the box, then spreads the two mats close together. We sit. She takes the box, opens it, hands me a rice ball and takes the other one for herself. We eat in silence. Finally, I have to ask her. "Your parents don't mind that I'm here?"

Keiko slowly shakes her head. "No."

"Okay." I'm still puzzled, but I accept her answer. I nod my head, and wonder what to say next. "Japan is very beautiful."

"Yes, very beautiful." Silence.

"Fuji is beautiful, the symbol of Japan."

"Yes." Silence.

"Do you work at the bar tonight?"

"No. No bar tonight. No bar tomorrow night, no bar next night." Suddenly she gets a shy look and asks, "Where you student?"

"A college on the East Coast of the United States."

"Why you not stay student?"

Good question. What *am* I doing here? Why am I not back at school, making the right friends and joining the right clubs? I think of my favorite place to study, a table in the library basement across from a large fresco, specifically a panel called *Gods of the Modern World*. From my chair, I could see skeletons in black academic robes delivering the bones of a fetus—a symbol of useless knowledge—from the pelvis of another grotesquely sprawled skeleton. For me, the ivory tower had become an ivory tomb, desiccated, devoid of *real* life. The skeletons whispered to me, telling me to flee, to go out and taste the world that lies beyond the stacks. Don't bury yourself in the dusty catacombs of senseless scholarship, they seemed to say. What's the value of a mental card catalogue of world literature to one who has never experienced the living source? And so, I fled.

How can I explain this to Keiko? I'll try. "In the school library, there's a painting of skeletons."

"Skeletons?"

"Bones and an empty skull. I don't want to be like the picture."

She looks blankly at me. "You come here from school?"

"Not exactly. First I worked. Many months, many jobs." I stop. It would take too long to explain. "I made just enough money to come here."

"You happy now?"

"Yes. I'm very happy now, right now. Right here, with you."

She smiles, then turns away from me and looks at Fuji-san. The sun sinks lower in the sky. Soon it will go behind the mountain. I reach out and touch her cheek. I look at her, seeking a clue, something to shake me out of my terrible indecisiveness. She turns to me, slowly lies back on her mat, reaches up and gently pulls me down next to her. We kiss. We kiss again.

"I am cat," Keiko whispers as she arches her back, runs her hand up beneath my shirt and lightly scratches my chest. Her fingers encounter my tiger tooth.

I pull it out from beneath my shirt to show her. "That's my good luck charm."

She nods, and gazes at me with intense seriousness. "I am cat," she repeats, and again runs her hand up under my shirt. Slowly she draws her nails down my chest and belly, then stops at my belt buckle. Suddenly, we hear voices, and the moment congeals. Two men are walking past us along a parallel berm about 30 feet away. Talking and laughing loudly, they don't seem to pay any attention to us. I can't understand a word they say, but of course Keiko can. She remains completely without expression, except for her eyes. She has a look I haven't seen before. Is it anger? Frustration? Defiance? She looks at me, and her eyes soften. She lays her head on my chest. The twilight deepens, and soon darkness settles on the green world around us.

Much later, we roll up the mats and again stroll along the dark berms. I have no idea where we are. Eventually, to my disappointment, we arrive back at Keiko's house. No lanterns are burning, inside or out. Keiko quietly steps up and slides open the screen. We tiptoe past the sleeping family and enter her darkened area of the house. I can't suppress a sigh.

I'd hoped we might find a room back in town, but I guess my hopes weren't realistic. I probably couldn't have paid for it anyway. I feel really clumsy, restrained by her family's presence, lost in this alien culture, surrounded by an ocean of rice fields. Keiko is very near me. I can't see her, but I hear her moving about. Suddenly a match flares. I hold my breath. She lights the tiny lantern and places it back on the small table. In the flickering orange glow, I confirm what I saw in the flare of the match. Keiko is naked.

She turns to face me. The lantern flickers quietly on the table. Tongues of orange light lick her body. Her eyes glisten as she stares at me. And waits.

The tincture of wisdom I possess urges caution with this girl whose bed pillow is inches away from her slumbering parents. But what are my choices? Stand here forever like a complete fool? Run out into the darkened rice paddies and drown myself? There she stands, naked in the shimmering lamplight, staring at me, waiting.

Okay. The worst they can do is kill me. Hopefully, not until morning. In two steps, I take her in my arms and press her to me. She raises her face, eyes closed, and we kiss. She opens her eyes and gives me a sweet smile.

Awkwardly, she fumbles with the buttons on my shirt. Gone is the teasing cat of the berms, changed into an infinitely tender, young woman. I step out of my jeans. She stoops, picks up our clothes and puts them in a corner. She blows out the lamp. In total darkness, we kiss again, and crawl into her bedchamber.

We're awake most of the night. She makes absolutely no effort to be quiet. Dawn is breaking when we finally fall asleep, her head next to mine on the pillow.

I wake up with a stab of fear in my gut. I'm alone in Keiko's bed, naked, and the fierce sunlight is again pouring through the gaps in the reed curtains. Fine! *Carpe Diem*, right? Ask any sophomore English major. "Now let us sport us while we may," says the poet. Great advice. Well, I sported. And where's it going to land me? Headless at the bottom of a rice paddy?

Images from my recent college class in Asian History swarm into my mind: photographs of Japanese soldiers beheading blindfolded prisoners, pictures of long trenches filled with the bodies of Chinese civilians, even pictures of people being buried alive while a group of Japanese soldiers stands around laughing and pointing. I remember stories of cannibalism by prison guards. By some accounts, the guards would actually cut off the flesh of a living prisoner, and then throw the mutilated body in a ditch to die. Am I going to end up the main ingredient for a couple hundred pieces of sushi? It's one thing to carry their daughter home in the midst of a typhoon. It's another thing entirely to keep the whole family awake all night with their daughter's sporting noises. And Keiko? What's going to happen to her?

I look at my watch; it's almost noon. Now what? Where is Keiko? Where's her dad? What should I do? Prepare to feebly defend myself against an enraged father and brother? I can hear them scream as they slice me to bits with their wicked swords. Or should I put on my clothes and creep out the door to vanish into the green mist? And never see Keiko again. In daylight, the sword scenario seems less probable. Surely, they would have killed me already. And to sneak away would be ignominious. One choice remains: Get dressed, sit down on the step, stare at the mountain, and await my fate. And hope that Keiko returns soon.

The green world is different today. I'm acutely conscious of each passing moment, and now I'm dreading the sound of the screen sliding open behind me.

Fuji looks different too: cold, cruel, indifferent to all human fate. I think of other Japanese volcanic mountains, especially Unzen in the Nagasaki prefecture, where for hundreds of years Christians—both Japanese and foreign—were tortured and killed by being thrown into the muddy, boiling, so-called *hells*, steaming pits filled with water heated to over 200 degrees Fahrenheit by the red-hot, molten lava surging below. A couple centuries later, the Christians retaliated against Nagasaki by blasting it with a modern form of fire, from the sky. What am I doing in the midst of this history?

Abruptly, the screen opens. I jerk my head around. There's Keiko's mother again, holding the same black lacquer tray with the teacup, chopsticks, and another fried egg. She kneels, places the tray next to me, and leaves without a word.

Keiko is an enigma. Now this is an enigma squared. Her parents must have heard us last night. No response. Where am I? In a parallel universe where the protocols of Cedar Grove don't exist? But philosophic speculation soon gives way to physical hunger. I wolf down the egg, savor the hot tea, and resume staring at the rice fields.

Keiko rounds a corner of the house and grins at me. "You finish?" she whispers. "Yes," I whisper back. She steps into the house with the tray and promptly returns. I take her hand, and we again enter the green world of rice and berms. This time we wander in a different direction from the prior day's walk. Eventually, the town appears in the distance. We walk past the railroad station and climb the hill to the central district.

In the marketplace, I buy an orange and two rice balls. Slowly we amble to the far edge of town, then sit on a small patch of grass and watch the puffs of white clouds float past the cone of Mt. Fuji. The mountain looks less threatening now. We finish our food without speaking. Keiko gives a happy sigh as I put my arm around her. We lie back on the grass and continue to watch the drifting clouds. As the sun begins to sink behind Fuji, we stroll back toward the marketplace.

I buy another orange. We sit on low stools and eat. Again, nobody seems to pay much attention to us. This really puzzles me because even in Tokyo, I had drawn many stares as the lone blond foreigner in the crowd.

The other people begin to disperse. Soon we're alone in the darkened marketplace. I can't figure out her family. They're practically invisible. Or maybe Keiko and I are the invisible ones. It's as if she lives alone in her tiny chamber.

I have to ask Keiko the question that's been on my mind since morning: "What about your parents? They must have heard us last night, but they haven't said a word."

Keiko is silent, ignoring my question.

I try again. "What do they think? How can they just not notice?" Still no response. "Keiko, do you understand my question?"

She silences me with a look. Then she kisses me. We sit and watch the stars come out. After a while, we walk back to her house and crawl into her bedroom. The night is too short.

We awake late the following morning. Her father and brother are still nowhere to be seen. Keiko and I again wander the berms and the town. We both know that I have to leave soon. At night, we return to her house and for the last time enter our own little world.

Our final night together. In the morning, I'll return to Tokyo. Our passion is tinged with sadness. Then, as the first light of dawn filters through the reeds, when we're lying in each other's arms, I feel her body tense. She abruptly pulls away. A look comes into her eyes that I've seen only once—on the path at twilight when the two men walked by. She stares hard at me.

"I am whore," she says, without a trace of emotion. I say nothing. "I am whore," she repeats, waiting for my response.

I'm not shocked, or really even surprised. This could explain a lot. But why is she telling me this now? I'm sure she isn't asking for money. She knows I don't have any. She isn't asking for anything, except my true feelings. I can only look at her. I feel a surge of protectiveness and tenderness. "Okay," is all I finally say. Then I kiss her.

The tension drains from her body and she melts into

me. We make love again, more strongly, yet more gently than before. Afterward, she sighs, closes her eyes, and hugs me tightly.

I begin to drift. She speaks my name once. We fall asleep in a close embrace.

When we awaken, the sun is rising over the rice fields. The mist-filtered rays slowly cover Mt. Fuji, turning the wooded slopes from black to green. Soon it will be time to go. I press her to me one last time. Our movements are slow and deliberate. We linger together longer than we should. I look at my watch. My train to Tokyo leaves in two hours. It's a long walk to the station. We crawl out of our enclosure, put on our clothes and leave the house.

With a few minutes to spare, we arrive at the station. We sit on a bench a few feet from the tracks and wait. Neither of us speaks. Soon we hear the train whistle in the distance and see the black smoke rising from the thundering locomotive. As the train approaches, we stand up. Keiko reaches into her kimono and brings out a small envelope. She presses it into my hand. I open the envelope. In it is a picture of her. The train screeches to a halt in front of the station. I now have her picture, but what can I give her? I have no photos or presents for her.

The train whistles. Passengers for the city begin to board. I reach up and remove my tiger tooth necklace, put it in her hand and quickly kiss her. She holds the chain up, smiles sadly, and puts it around her neck.

The engine groans and pours out clouds of smoke. The train begins to move. I jump aboard the last car as it pulls away from the station. Keiko stands and watches. I lose sight of her as we round a curve and head toward Tokyo.

The train jostles and clatters along the tracks. I pull out Keiko's picture and stare at the black and white image of her, standing alone. What is she thinking now? What's going to happen to her? I never lied to Keiko. I gave her no false expectations. I'll always remember her. But what was I, really, to her? Just some idiot who blundered into her life for a few days and wobbled about, caught between testosterone and terror? Could I possibly have given her as much as she gave me? And I still can't figure out her parents. Jari Keranen, you sweet, little Finnish boy. Such a pity you're mentally deficient.

Slumped in my gloomy self-doubt, I barely notice the movement of the train until it finally slows, then clunks and squeals into the Tokyo station. So what should I tell Bill? Probably best to leave things vague. Just say I had an interesting time.

I walk from the station to our hotel. It's long past noon, but Bill is still sleeping. I wake him up, and we head for our favorite coffee house. The waitress serves us iced coffees, and Bill's head finally begins to clear from his revelry of the night before. He looks at me with a benevolent, yet condescending smile.

"So, college boy. Good to see you survived your foray into postwar, rural Japan. I placed the odds at 50-50."

"Yeah. No problems, really. I guess I was just lucky."

"So what did you do?"

"Nothing much. Just wandered around."

Bill sips his iced coffee, and gives me a skeptical look. "I see. Just wandered around?"

"Uh huh. Just wandered around."

"You've been awake for five days?"

"No."

"Where did you sleep?"

"On a railroad station bench."

"Five nights on a bench? How romantic."

"Not five nights. Just one."

"And the rest?"

"On the floor."

"What floor?"

"Does it matter?"

"Why are you being so cagey?" He takes another sip of coffee, and then smiles. "Come on kid. Stop jousting. What's the big secret?"

I can't help it. I really do want to tell him. I want him to see the beauty, the mystery, and the wistfulness of the whole experience. "Well, the first night in the town, I had a beer in a bar. These two women came over to talk to me, and—"

"Ah ha! I thought you said you were low on cash."

"I was. I am. But what does that have to do with anything?"

"Nothing. Sorry, kid. I'll shut up. Go on."

So I tell him the whole story. Bill listens quietly as I relate my tale. I conclude with, "It was really beautiful." Then I show him Keiko's picture. I sip my iced coffee and wait for his response.

He says nothing for a time, and then slowly shakes his head in apparent disbelief. "Oh, my God," he finally mutters. "Are you naïve, college boy. The only thing in your pants that a whore cares about is your wallet."

"That's not true in this case," I argue, stung by his cynicism.

"Look kid, her parents obviously forced her to earn her keep as a whore."

"Bill! She knew from day *one* that I had almost no money. She wouldn't even let me buy her a drink!"

Bill just continues to shake his head. "Naïve, naïve. Look, college boy, some poor families even sell their daughters to brothels. Sounds like her family's just renting her out."

"That's really cynical, Bill, even for you."

"I'm sorry, kid. I'm not trying to hurt your feelings."

"Bill, she never asked for money, she never expected money. I don't care if you believe it or not. She had a kind of fearlessness; she gave herself completely to the moment, to the feeling, to me. She asked for nothing and gave everything. She's a wonderful woman. And I was her lover, her real lover, for a brief, beautiful moment."

"Sure you were, college boy. And by the way, 'lover' is a really old-fashioned word."

"Look, Bill, when she was lying in my arms and told me she was a prostitute, that wasn't a request for money."

"Then why'd she do it?"

"Why? That's obvious! She wanted to know if I would still like her, if I could still respect her, still love her. And she found out that I could, that our time together was honest and beautiful."

"Sure, sure it was," he nods.

"Bill, nobody will ever convince me that all during those days and nights, Keiko secretly despised me as a mere *gaijin* john who was going to pay her for the use of her body. Besides, to look for romance and beauty in life is not naïveté." This earnest declaration quiets Bill for a moment, but doesn't put a dent in his profound skepticism.

"Well, okay college boy, if you say so." And he knocks back the rest of his coffee.

"Look, all she ever took from me was my good luck tiger tooth."

Bill just nods. I finish my coffee, and we walk out into the frantic streets of Tokyo.

Many months later. It's bleak mid-winter in frozen New Hampshire. I'm back in the basement of the college library. When I returned a few months ago, the black-robed skeletons on the wall greeted me with malicious grins. Welcome home, they sneered. Welcome back to your comfortable ivory tomb. So glad to see you, they hissed. Now, do your homework, write your papers, and build the foundation for your own smug certainty of the inevitable rightness of your scholarly opinions. In the future, confine your wanderings to the dusty temples of our elevated, intellectual world, cushioned from the beastly brawling of the groundlings massed outside our fortress.

But now the image of the black-robed specters is often blurred, sometimes almost erased, by the image of Keiko in our private world surrounded by a shimmering green sea of rice paddies. I can still see her weaving down the muddy road in the typhoon. I can feel the touch of her fingers on my lips. Her scent, her body heat, and the look that I first saw in her eyes on the berm when the laughing yokels wounded her with some jibe—everything is fresh in my mind. And the final image of her pressing her picture into my hand, then standing alone watching as the Tokyo train took me away. I carry her picture with me. I will never forget her.

This evening, the skeletons in their somber academic robes stare at me with particular malevolence. What if Bill was right? What if it *was* all a lie? A charade in which I played the innocent fool. I close my books and stuff them into my backpack.

Outside, it's bitter cold and snowing, a dusky landscape of deserted streets flanked by dormitories housing lonely young men. I zip my jacket and wrap my scarf tightly around my neck, then trudge through the snow back to my dorm. In my mailbox is a letter from Bill. I slowly walk upstairs to my room. From my window, as the twilight fades, I watch the snowflakes drift silently down onto the desolate streets below. I turn on my desk lamp and open the letter.

I can hear Bill's voice and see him sipping his coffee as he writes:

Hi, college boy,

I'll probably stay here in Japan for another few months 'til my money runs out. Then I'll have to go back to the States and work to save up some more cash. Tokyo hasn't changed. As crazy and exciting as ever. How's life back in the library?
Bill

P.S. I took a trip to Fuji-san about a week ago. Found your favorite bar and actually met Keiko. Had a beer with her. I told her I was your friend. Guess what, college boy. She's still wearing your necklace.

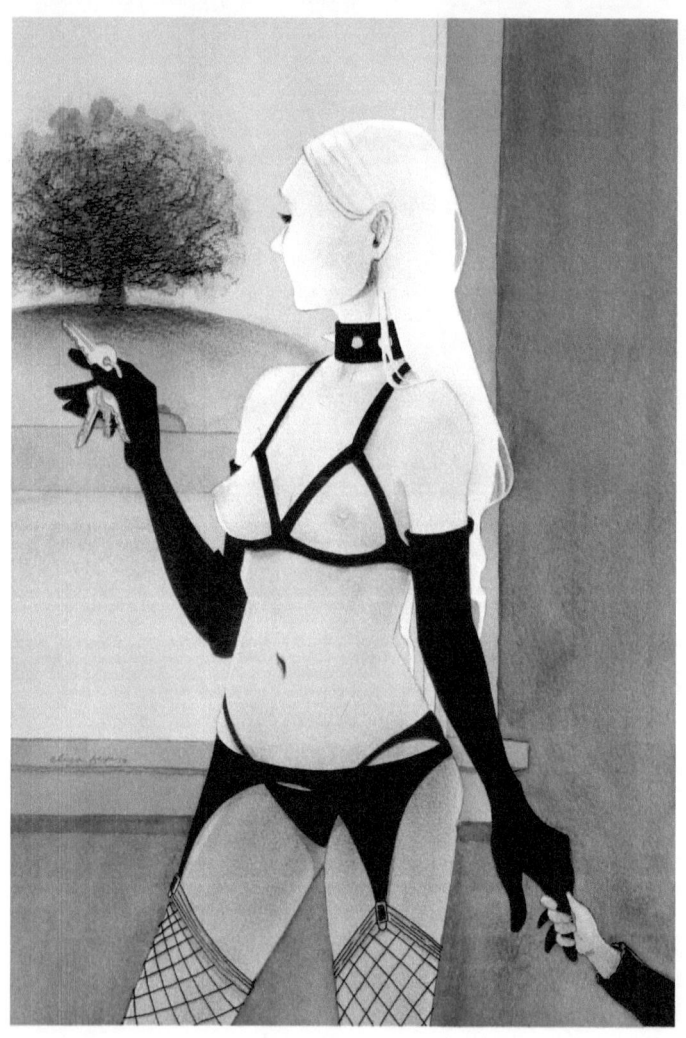

PING—CLICK

A soft *click*. The ratchet tightened. Then *ping—click*. Steel on steel. Again *click, ping—click*. More steel. Silence. Then again, *click, ping—click. Click, ping—click*. Silence.

Tassie Bruner lay naked on her stomach, spread-eagled across the sheets, wrists and ankles securely cuffed to the heavy steel bedstead. Her husband, Hank, knelt above her. Slowly, he began to stroke himself as he quietly surveyed her pale, defenseless body.

Sweat. The air was heavy, steamy, dense with the smell of sweat mingled with a faint burning odor from the red-hot heat lamp placed on a wooden box and trained on Hank's precious pot plants. And fear. Hank knew the smell of fear. Kneeling between her outstretched legs, he reached out to roughly squeeze her buttocks with his right hand, and made himself hard with his left. Tassie didn't move. She kept her eyes tightly closed. Abruptly, Hank stretched his sweaty body over Tassie and entered her. In a moment, it was all over. He collapsed atop Tassie's still form. "Beautiful," he whispered, "really kinky." Tassie said nothing. Her eyes remained closed. Slowly, Hank freed her wrists and ankles, then flopped back on the bed and fell asleep. Tassie lay silently on the damp sheets. As Hank began to snore, she opened her eyes. Her thin brown hair hung limp and lifeless across her shoulders. The night wind sighed and rustled the tall grass in the meadow surrounding their tiny, wooden farmhouse about two miles west of town.

Hank snored and tossed for the usual two hours. Then, when the pot and the alcohol and the post-coital drowse began to wear off, he gave a snort and his eyes popped open. Hank stared through the gloom at the ceiling fan slowly turning above the bed. He tried hard to focus on just one blade, to follow the tip around a complete revolution, to cut all memory out with the slowly spinning blade. No good. The fan blades were going just a little too fast for the eye to follow, and he would lose the tip again and again and again. Hank rolled over onto his stomach, closed his eyes, and listened to the soft hum of the fan motor as it spun the blades around in their seemingly eternal orbit.

Seven a.m. the following morning. Tassie stood alone at the stove. Near her on the white Formica counter, cooked bacon lay draining on a paper napkin. Their two-year-old son, Luke, sat in his highchair watching her while she fried Hank's eggs. As the grease popped and sizzled in the pan, Tassie stared through the grimy kitchen window at an ancient California black oak growing in the field behind the house. Deeply rooted down to bedrock, the tree stood alone. Towering, enduring, unyielding. However, though black oaks can live for 500 years, the trunks are often decayed and hollow.

For the past month, every morning since it happened, Tassie had replayed the same scene in her mind. She saw herself standing rigid at the window, Luke clutched tightly to her breast, watching Hank, chain in hand, beneath the tree. And the Doberman. Inside the house, the sound of the dog's cries had been muted. This had served to emphasize the dreamlike rhythm of Hank's powerful arm as it rose and descended like an oil rig along a California desert highway, a terrible engine of pain, rising and falling, the bundle of torn flesh on the ground slowly becoming a blood-drenched pulp. Frozen, Tassie had watched. And then, she'd made up her mind. *You've got to do it, girl. You have no choice.* The dog had continued to howl.

Tassie looked back at the frying pan. "Hank! Your eggs are ready."

"Be there in a sec," he boomed from the bathroom.

Hank Bruner was a cop—in his own way, an effective cop—recently promoted to plainclothes detective. Six foot three, heavily muscled, blond hair cut close, thin mustache carefully trimmed, he stood with shoulders back, feet slightly apart, nonchalantly displaying the faint bulge of the gun in his shoulder holster. The bad guys didn't want to tangle with him, yet the good citizens who passed what Hank called "the attitude test" found him polite, friendly, often charming. But even the most attitudinally correct folks sensed the barely restrained violence hidden behind his casual, smiling exterior. Hank's father, an army sergeant, had raised Hank carefully, applying with a practiced hand the discipline necessary to properly train a youthful recruit. Hank's mother, a field mouse of a woman, rarely spoke.

Hank's only peccadillo vis-à-vis the law was his indoor marijuana farming. Tassie disapproved. "You're a cop, for god's sake," Tassie often said. "Cops shouldn't be growing pot in their bedroom. And the goddamn heat lamp. You're going to burn the house down!" But Hank ignored his wife's concerns. He found it much safer to grow his own weed rather than buy it from the "scumbag perps" he routinely busted. Besides, the heat lamp served a dual purpose. He liked to sweat during sex. It had a cleansing effect.

Tassie put the bacon and eggs on a plate and brought them over to the table. Hank entered the kitchen with a smile. "How do you like the suit, hon? Now, no one can see me coming." He bent over and kissed her forehead. Next to Hank, five-foot-two, 105-pound Tassie looked like a miniature woman.

"The suit's lovely, Hank," Tassie murmured as she set a bowl of oatmeal in front of Luke.

Hank placed his pistol on top of the refrigerator and sat down to breakfast. "I actually slept a bit last night, honey." He winked and gave her a knowing smile.

Tassie sat down next to Luke. "I'm glad you did, Hank." She began to carefully feed the child small amounts of oatmeal.

"Hey! How many times do I have to tell you! Let the kid feed himself. He's big enough."

"Sure Hank, then you get upset when he spills a little." *Careful. Don't get him started.*

"He has to learn good table manners."

"He's only two."

"He has to learn!" Hank grabbed the spoon from Tassie's hand and stuck it in the bowl in front of Luke. "Now feed yourself. And don't spill. Got that?"

Uncertain, Luke looked at Hank, then at Tassie. "It's okay, Luke. You heard Daddy. Do as he says." Luke hesitated, and then carefully picked up the spoon. He held it clumsily and dipped it into the oatmeal. "Just take a very small bite, sweetheart," Tassie said. The child took a bit of oatmeal, and got most of it into his mouth.

"See, Tassie? I told you. Good boy, Luke."

Hank wolfed down the last of his eggs and bacon. He carefully wiped his mouth with a paper napkin, then glared at Tassie. "By the way, who were you talking to yesterday afternoon?"

Tassie was puzzled. "Who?"

"You know who. Who was that guy?"

"What guy?"

"The guy in the grocery store parking lot." Tassie had to think for a moment. *The parking lot. But how does Hank know?* "Quit stalling! Who was he?"

"Oh, you must mean Stanley. He's just a guy I went to high school with."

"Oh yeah? Well, I don't like him. Stay away from him."

"Hank, I haven't seen him for years. I just ran into him yesterday."

"Was he your boyfriend?"

"No. Just a friend. An acquaintance really. After high school, he went east to college, then stayed there. He just came back here a few days ago to visit his family."

Hank grunted. "Well, just be careful. You never know who's watching you."

Suddenly, Hank stood up. Luke stopped eating and stared at his father, looking for any further cues. Hank walked slowly over to the refrigerator. "Don't wait up for me tonight, Tassie. Got a busy day. An afternoon court appearance. The fat-assed lawyer I stopped for speeding and reckless driving a while ago when I was still in uniform. That fucker sure failed the attitude test. A real wise-ass. Big fucking attorney, thinks I won't show up in court, thinks he'll beat the ticket. Cocksucker. He'll see. This little tickey is gonna stick."

"What's on after the court appearance?"

"A few beers with some friends. We made plans to go to the City afterward." Tassie knew what that meant: a boy's night out cruising the San Francisco bondage scene.

Hank grabbed his gun, carefully set it in his holster, then walked over and tickled Luke under the chin. He gave Tassie a wink and a peck on the cheek, and strode to the front door. After sliding back the deadbolt, he detached the twin chain locks, opened the door and turned to Tassie. "Oh, Tassie, you know if I ever catch you seeing another guy, I'll break your legs."

Tassie was silent.

"Just kidding," Hank said with a smile as he closed the door behind him.

When she heard Hank's car start, Tassie picked up the spoon and resumed feeding Luke.

Shortly before they were married, Hank had taken Tassie to a San Francisco bondage club. He told her that he liked women who were really "kinky," like some of the women in the club. Tassie was by no means a prude, but she witnessed things that evening that she doubted she would ever like to experience. She couldn't imagine herself enjoying the restraints, paddles, switches, clamps, and most of the other equipment involved in S&M pleasures.

In the car on the way home, Hank had been annoyed. "Don't be so squeamish, Tassie. You think anyone is forced to go to a club?"

"I don't know what to think, Hank."

"Well, they're not forced. They enjoy it. It's a kick. Nobody really gets hurt."

"It's just new to me, that's all."

"Okay, Tassie. Fine. Nobody's going to make you do anything you don't want to do." They'd driven the rest of the way home in silence.

Hank had kept his word. Just give her time, he'd figured. And sure enough, last night she'd finally come around. By agreeing to the four-point restraints, Tassie had proven her adaptability

Since the Doberman incident, Tassie had learned a great deal more about Hank's nocturnal city adventures. The evening after Hank had buried the dog, Tassie began to reveal her change of heart. She'd snuggled next to Hank on the couch, playfully tickled his ear, and whispered, "You know, Hank, maybe I'll go with you again to one of those clubs."

"Are you serious?" Hank was suspicious, yet a spark of hope flashed within him. "I thought you said the clubs weren't for you."

"I'm not saying I'll go with you all the time," laughed Tassie. "Just call it curiosity."

Hank was pleased. At last, she was starting to see things his way. *Well, it took her long enough.* "Are you sure this is what you want?" he demanded, narrowing his eyes and carefully appraising his wife.

"Why not?" she said with a smile. "Let's just say you've got my attention."

A few days later, they went to a club. Tassie stayed the whole evening with no complaints, and carefully observed everything. She wasn't sure what Hank did when he went there without her, but she forced herself not to think about it, not to care. As the month wore on, she accompanied Hank a couple more times, always observing, learning new things, learning what really turned him on. Hank's doubts subsided, and he began to view Tassie with a certain puzzled respect. Finally, last night, she let him realize some of his dreams with her.

Hank and Tassie had gotten married as soon as Hank's divorce was final, about six years after the Vietnam war ended. Tassie was working as a bookkeeper at a downtown department store, a job that didn't much thrill her, and still living with her parents. She'd wanted to be a nurse, but could never afford the schooling. As a little girl, Tassie brought home every wounded bird and ailing small creature that she could find. One day, she even brought home a worm, half of which had been run over by a passing bicycle. The flat part of the worm was motionless, but the round part was very active indeed. What should she do? Cut the flat part off? Maybe the wound would heal, and the worm would just be shorter? Or leave the flat part on, and hope it would be okay in the morning? Tassie decided against the surgery. She gently put the creature in a shoebox and carefully covered it with a thin layer of moist, dark earth from the vegetable garden behind the house. The following morning, Tassie discovered that the problem was solved. The round previously active part of the worm was no longer moving. Nothing she tried could revive it. After school that day, she reverently buried the remains next to a row of carrots in the garden.

Prior to Hank, Tassie's relationships with men had been equally disappointing. "Why do you always bring home the stray dogs, the weakest of the litter?" her father frequently asked her. She said she didn't know. But she was tired of "babies who wanted a mommy to take care of them," as her mother often put it. Tassie wanted a change.

She decided that if she presented a more adventurous image, it might help to attract a sturdier type of male. Tassie got her parents to help her buy an old Jeep. She then found a suitably distressed pair of cowboy boots and a few flannel shirts at a local thrift shop. Faded jeans completed her new wardrobe. One final touch: Tassie had her hair stylist give her a platinum streak, just the right amount for that slightly edgy quality. She began to frequent the local bars with her girlfriends on weekends.

One Saturday night, Tassie met Hank Bruner at the Bar Texas. The saloon's dim interior contained a long, dark hardwood bar with a series of taps featuring a variety of beers ranging from Guinness to Bud Light. The mirrored backbar held glass shelves filled with various colorful bottles. Tassie and a friend took two stools close to the entrance. Round, dark tables were set against the wall opposite the bar. A single red-shaded pin spot hung above each table. Neon beer signs covered the walls, a visual cacophony, each sign stridently competing for the attention of the thirsty customers. The place had a permanent aroma of greasy hamburgers and stale popcorn. Classic rock and country music blared from the jukebox.

At the last table in the far corner, Hank sat with a couple of friends, his back to the wall. Tassie quickly spotted him. "Oh, look at that one," she murmured to her friend, a big-boned, bubbly brunette.

"Which one?"

"The guy way down at the end, the last table."

"You mean the big guy with the mustache?"

"Yeah. Pity he's so far away."

"Try the magnet, Tassie baby."

Tassie took a sip of her draft Heineken and stared over the lip of the glass at Hank. In a few seconds, Hank abruptly looked up. He quickly scanned the room and locked eyes with Tassie. She set her beer on the bar and smiled. A few moments later, Hank stood up and strolled over to the two women.

"Good evening, ladies," he said, bowing slightly.

"My, aren't we chivalrous," laughed Tassie.

Hank smiled and nodded. "I've seen you around town," he said with a big grin. "You drive an old red Jeep and wear cowboy boots."

"You're very observant."

"Why thank you, ma'am."

"I don't recall seeing you, sir."

"Of course not. On duty, I'm invisible. All people see is the car."

"The car?"

"Yeah. It's black and white with Christmas lights on top. Can't miss it."

Tassie laughed. "Christmas lights. You're a cop."

"At your service, ma'am. Would you ladies care to join me and my friends?"

"Sure, why not," Tassie said, flashing a radiant smile. Hank picked up their drinks and politely ushered the women to his table.

Hank's surface charm and obvious physical strength had strongly attracted Tassie. Even today, she smiled at the memory of Hank's quaint discussion with her parents not long after she met him.

Tassie was upstairs coaxing her hair into a suitably durable style for the evening. The doorbell rang. "I'll get it," her mother yelled up the stairwell. Mrs. Daniels, a warm-hearted dumpling of a woman who perpetually reeked of cheap, floral perfume, walked briskly to the front door and opened it. There in the twilight stood Hank. He wore a dark suit and carried a bunch of yellow roses.

"Good evening, Mrs. Daniels." Hank's easy smile carried a slight hint of nervousness, which only increased his charm. "If you have a little time, I'd like to speak to you and Mr. Daniels." He then presented the thoroughly captivated mother with the roses.

"Who is it, Mom?" Tassie called from the top of the stairs. She knew perfectly well that it was Hank, since she could hear everything that happened below.

"It's Hank, dear. Take your time. You want to look your best, you know," answered Mrs. Daniels, giving Hank a coy smile. She ushered him into the living room where Mr. Daniels sat sipping a Bristol Cream as he read through a back issue of *The Economist*.

Mr. Wilbur Daniels had met his wife Martha in a business class at Chico State. They got married, and soon afterward Tassie was born. Martha had come to California to escape life on a small farm in Tennessee. She figured her five brothers could handle the chores without her. Wilbur had visions of launching a successful business in his hometown near Sonoma. Although he wasn't sure what kind of business, he'd felt stirrings of the entrepreneurial spirit while he and Martha were living on loans from their parents. Thirty years later, he was resigned to ending his career as the manager of a local big-box store.

"Hank, it's good to see you again," said Mr. Daniels, rising and warmly shaking Hank's hand. "Please sit down." He gestured Hank toward a brown leather armchair on the other side of the glass coffee table in front of the couch. "Martha, how about a sherry for this young man?"

"Oh, no thank you, Mr. Daniels. I'm fine."

"Perhaps a beer or something?" enquired Mrs. Daniels,

dimly aware of the faint touch of condescension in her question.

"No, thank you, Mrs. Daniels," answered Hank, his easy smile unbroken. "Tassie and I will have wine with dinner."

Mr. and Mrs. Daniels sat down on the couch. Mrs. Daniels still clutched the bouquet of yellow roses. The three smiled at one another.

Abruptly, Hank blurted out the reason behind his request for an audience. "Mr. and Mrs. Daniels, I've come to ask you for Tassie's hand in marriage. She and I have already discussed the matter." Hank's archaic formality suggested a careful rehearsal.

"Oh my," said Mrs. Daniels, raising a hand to her lips.

"Well, well, you young people don't waste any time, do you," said Mr. Daniels.

Upstairs, Tassie continued to fix her hair before wriggling into her signature tight jeans. By the time she bounced downstairs, her cowboy boots clacking on the hardwood steps, parental permission had been granted.

"My, don't we look comfortable tonight, dear," said Mrs. Daniels, looking with disapproval at her daughter's casual attire. Tassie glanced quizzically at Hank's dark suit.

"I thought I'd give you a little surprise tonight, hon,"

said Hank, in his deepest masculine tones. We're dining at Bella Italia." Hank shook Mr. Daniels's hand, nodded politely to Mrs. Daniels, and ushered Tassie out to his black Chevy convertible.

"A breath of fresh air," said her father.

"At last, someone she won't have to coddle," her mother added.

An hour later, over candlelight, a bottle of Chianti, and plates of spaghetti, Tassie and Hank discussed their future. She sat with her elbows on the table, leaning forward, eyes wide, intent on Hank's every word. At one point, she decided to touch on a subject that she sensed was somehow forbidden.

"Hank, you haven't told me anything about Vietnam. What did you do there, in the war?"

Hank swallowed a forkful of pasta and sipped his wine. "I spent a lot of time alone in the jungle."

"What was it like?"

"I can't remember."

"You can't remember anything?"

"No. When I got home, I took those years and stuffed them into a duffle bag. Then I wrapped the bag in chains and threw it in an attic closet." Hank signaled the waitress. "Another bottle of wine, please." Then he looked hard at Tassie. "And don't *ever* ask me about the war again."

Suddenly, Hank blushed a deep red. His eyes watered. He reached across the table and gently took Tassie's hand. "I'm sorry, honey. I don't mean to be harsh. It's just—it's just that things happen—things you don't want, that you never wanted. But they happen. And then, you can't take them back. You're still alive. That's all you know."

"That's okay, Hank. I'm sorry I was so, I don't know … nosey."

Hank picked up his wine glass and twirled it slowly in front of the candle. He stared at the swirling red liquid, and for a full minute, he left Tassie, the table, the restaurant, the town, and went far, far away. Abruptly, he blinked. He knocked back the wine, and set the glass firmly on the table. "Last word. If you weren't there, you'll never understand. End of discussion."

"It's okay, darling, whatever happened."

Hank nodded his head, once. "We're here today, and you're so precious to me. I refuse to focus on the past. I only care about the future, our future, together. I'll do whatever it takes to protect you."

For a big man, Hank had delicate hands. His caress

could be as light as a feather, soft, tender. He leaned forward, raised Tassie's hand to his lips, and kissed it. "Our future, together, begins tonight."

Tassie smiled. "You were so cute with my parents."

Hank released her hand as the waitress arrived with their second bottle of wine. "I know we don't need anyone's permission to get married. But I want everything to be just right for us. I guess I'm a little old fashioned."

"That's one of the things I love about you."

"Oh, there are others?"

"I think I've already shown you the answer to that question."

Hank laughed. "Yeah. I guess so. And a very impressive display it was." He raised his glass. "Here's to good questions—and answers."

As Tassie sipped her wine, she realized that she had never felt so loved, so sheltered, as she did by this strong man whom she knew she loved in return. Her heart gave a little flutter. Finally, Tassie was at peace.

And concerning the war, it was settled between them. It was official. Hank had forgotten Vietnam: the oppressive heat, the lack of sleep, the endless rain, the stench of burning bodies, the blood, the muck, the crushing fatigue as he labored through the swamps with his heavy pack, the snakes, the spiders, the scorpions, the swarms of mosquitoes, the thousand other stinging and biting jungle insects, the oozing sores on his feet and legs, the vast green waves of razor-sharp elephant grass, the screams of landmine victims, the smoke, the thunder of artillery, the bombs, the napalm fires, the darkness, the foul water, the leeches, the crotch rot, the sweat, the sudden storms, the snipers, the moans of his wounded buddies, the rice paddies, the burning metal of grenade fragments slicing through his flesh, the booby traps, the flare bursts, the sound of helicopters, the flaming huts, the adrenaline rush of sudden violence, the constant sense of slogging through a foggy nightmare in a matrix of endless suffering. And, of course, the things without a name. They, too, got stuffed in the duffle. But the things without a name would not be contained. They sifted through the rotting fiber, glided silently beneath the closet door and drifted out of the attic, will-o-the-wisps, persistent, intent on following Hank, day and night, wherever he might go.

Hank did make it to court for the hearing on the attorney's ticket. And the citation did stick.

After breakfast the following morning, he glanced

warily around him before entering his unmarked white cruiser. As he warmed up the car's engine, he stared at his face in the rearview mirror for a long moment. *Christ! I look like a goddamn raccoon! Gotta get more sleep.* But Hank knew he wouldn't. *So what's next, the needle? Shut up, idiot. You've seen what the needle did to a couple of your buddies. Got home safe. A few years later, both dead.* Hank knew he would never use the needle. He would tough it out alone, as he always had before.

Hank jammed the car into gear and bounced down the dirt road, turned right onto the highway, and headed into town. He liked the wide meadows and the gently rolling hills in the distance. He could always see what was coming at him.

He passed the four corners and glanced up at a faint plume of gray smoke coming from Nate Matlock's place, a tiny cabin perched at the very top of a round, grassy hill about a half mile away. Hank pitied the man. *Poor old Nate, the local hermit. Came home from Korea back in the 50s minus one leg. And maybe minus his mind. Built a shack on his parent's farm, and stayed home. Never left. Except he comes into town every Christmas eve to the Bar Texas. Gets roaring drunk. Before he passes out, he starts babbling and raving about peace on earth, about human wave attacks, enemy bodies stacked up to the sky, machine gun barrels so hot they melted, had to fall back, took one in the knee. Knocked his goddamn leg off. Poor bastard.*

As Hank cruised past El Portal Road, he remembered his last traffic stop on his final day in uniform. Hank was off on the shoulder, parked in the shade of a big Eucalyptus tree. A young guy in a beat-up old green Ford had come to a rolling stop, then turned quickly onto the highway. Hank had flipped on his Christmas lights and pulled the kid over. He approached the car on the passenger side. "Good morning, sir," Hank said.

"Good morning, officer."

"You always roll through stop signs?"

"No, sir, I don't think so. I guess I must have rolled through the last one, huh? I apologize."

"May I see your driver's license, sir?"

"Sure." He fished it out of his wallet and handed it across to Hank.

"Mr. William Henry. Is this your current address?"

"No, sir. I cancelled the lease before I left."

"Left for where?

"My unit was sent to Lebanon. Beirut. Just got back a week ago. I'm looking for work, so for now I'm staying with my parents here in town."

Hank moved around to the driver's window, noting that the fellow had again placed both hands on the steering wheel. "Okay," Hank said as he handed back the driver's license. "Welcome home, soldier. Next time, remember you're back home in little old U.S. of A. And here's a present for you." Hank handed him a card with the words "Have a Nice Day" printed over a smiley face.

"Thank you, officer. I'll be more careful."

"You're a civilian now. Gotta act like one."

The driver nodded in agreement. Hank returned to his car and watched the ex-soldier slowly pull back onto the highway and drive off.

Hank smiled at the memory as he turned right onto Main Street, and cruised slowly past the antique shops and the crowded cafes. Two more right turns and he'd looped back onto Cleveland Avenue. More antique shops, salons, and cafes. *Shit! This place is becoming a goddamn yuppie bin.*

A middle-aged Asian woman and a young girl about nine or ten years old came out of a nail salon, and walked down the sidewalk toward Hank. The little girl had long, straight, black hair and huge, dark, almond eyes. Hank looked away. That's when he spotted the red-faced guy in a tattered, khaki raincoat sitting cross-legged on the pavement in front of the bookstore. Hank turned to the curb and parked in a red zone. The seated man stared down at the sidewalk while he shook a paper coffee cup with a few coins in it. *Homeless guys— a bunch of wackos and druggies. They give the town an unsafe feeling. Their scraggly beards, blood-shot eyes, rotted teeth, foul breath, grimy hands with broken fingernails—disgusting. They make me sick. I don't want Luke growing up with these bums around.*

Hank got out of the car, strolled over and stood in front of the seated figure. "Time to move along, buddy."

The cup stopped shaking, but the man kept staring at the sidewalk. "It's a free country."

Oh, how Hank loved to hear *that* line. "Yeah, and I'm telling you to be free somewhere else."

The man looked up slowly. "Who are you?"

"I'm the guy telling you to get your ass off this public thoroughfare and get the hell out of here."

"You some kinda cop in a cheap suit? Got a badge?"

Oh boy, this guy's really failed the attitude test. Big time. Hank smiled as he flashed his wallet. "On your feet, citizen. Now! Let's see your ID."

"What am I doin' wrong?"

"Well, citizen, we have laws against aggressive panhandling and obstructing a public walkway. And by the way, have you been drinking? We also have laws against public drunkenness. Now stand up and show me some ID."

"Asshole," the man muttered as he stood up.

"What'd you say?"

"Nothin'."

"That's funny. I could swear you called me an asshole. That's insulting a police officer in the performance of his duty. And disturbing the peace. And since you haven't shown me your ID, that's failure to obey a lawful order from a police officer. Keep talking."

That's when raincoat man made his big mistake. He tried to shove Hank out of the way and run down the alley next to the store. He didn't get very far.

That evening, Hank was in high spirits. Over a steak dinner, he described the raincoat man scene to Tassie. "I sure fixed his wagon," Hank laughed as he stuffed a thick piece of beef into his mouth. He chewed it greedily, washed it down with half a can of beer, then expressed his approval with a flamboyant belch.

"Whose wagon did you fix, dear?" *Be careful, girl.*

Hank shot her a glance. *Is she being sarcastic? Making fun of me? Look at her blank face and big brown eyes. She better watch herself.* "He was a big son-of-a-bitch," Hank answered slowly. "Guess he thought he was pretty tough. I grabbed him by the coat collar, and somehow—accidentally, of course—he tripped, and his face got rubbed along the nice rough cinder block wall for about six feet. He wasn't too pretty after that. So there he was. I added assaulting a police officer and resisting arrest to the list of charges. Then I took him to the station and threw him in a cell. That prick made my day."

That night, it was a full moon. After dinner, Hank smoked a few joints and drank a six-pack of beer. Tassie put Luke to bed, washed the dishes, brushed her teeth, and crawled into bed beside Hank. "Hey, hon, Luke's asleep," Hank whispered. "How about a quickie?"

Afterward, Hank collapsed and started to snore. In a while, the snoring stopped. For a time, he lay completely still. Hardly breathing. Then he started to tremble. Tassie turned over and watched him. In the moonlight, she could see he had both hands up around his throat. He looked like he was trying to strangle himself. And he was crying, making little squeaky noises, like a tiny animal caught in a trap. His eyes were half open, but she knew he wasn't awake. She wanted to touch him, to make the nightmare go away, to help him, but she was afraid. He'd warned her their first night together never to wake him up suddenly. Said he might hurt her, a sort of reflex, that maybe he couldn't stop himself in time. Suddenly, Hank groaned and sat up. Tassie closed her eyes. Hank slowly lay back down and stared at the ceiling fan.

The following day, after Hank left, Tassie phoned her mother.

"Why are you calling, dear? You sound worried."

Careful, Tassie. Don't tell her too much too soon. Remember, need to know is all she gets. Tassie frowned. *Need to know. One of Hank's favorite phrases.* "I'm worried about Hank, Mom."

"Now, dear, we've discussed this before. We know it's sometimes difficult to be a policeman's wife."

"Mom, his being a cop isn't the problem."

Mrs. Daniels sighed. "All right, dear, tell me what the trouble is now."

"It's not his job, Mom. It's something else, maybe the war, something he won't talk about."

"Darling, the war was a long time ago. No, it's just the stress of his job."

"That's not true, Mom. I'm telling you, he's a time

bomb. You remember how he told me that when he became a plain clothes cop, he could follow me around and I wouldn't know it?"

"Yes, Tassie, I remember, like the time he followed you out to that country bakery. But that was before he got out of uniform, wasn't it?"

"He was off duty, Mom."

"He just wanted to protect you, Tassie."

"From scones and sticky buns? Mom, it's not what you think. He seems to follow me all the time now."

"Oh, Tassie, you're just imagining things."

"No, I'm not. I think he has the idea that I'm seeing someone else."

Mrs. Daniels was silent for a moment. "Well … are you … involved with someone, dear?"

"No, Mom, you know I love Hank. But I don't know what to do. I knew he had some problems before I married him, but I thought I could help. I hoped he'd open up to me and we could solve them together. But it's not working out that way."

"He won't talk to you?"

"No. And he gets angry no matter what I say. And I'm really worried about Luke." Tassie started to cry. "Mom, I don't want to desert Hank, like his first wife did. But I'm afraid of what he might to do to me, even to Luke."

"Tassie, darling, don't let your imagination carry you away. Things will change. Just be patient. And when you need to talk, call me. You can always confide in me."

But Tassie knew that wasn't true. Her parents knew next to nothing about her marriage. Or her life, her real life, even before her marriage. She had made sure of that. Why disturb their comfort? They wouldn't understand anyway. "Okay, Mom, I'll keep trying. But I know he's going to explode someday. And I don't want to be there with Luke when it happens."

Tassie hung up the phone and walked slowly out to the kitchen. She filled a glass with water from the faucet and looked out the window at the solitary oak tree. *Time and distance. Time and distance. All right, girl. Don't stop now.*

Sunday afternoon football, the TV blaring. The roar of the Los Angeles crowd filled the stadium and Tassie's living room. A diehard Oakland Raiders fan, Hank had stuck with them even after they'd moved to L.A. He loved football, but he refused to go to a live game because he couldn't tolerate mobs of people. Strictly a living room quarterback, he sat on the couch, leaning forward, eagerly watching the players' every move. Two or three joints had gone up in smoke. A jumble of empty beer cans lay crumpled on the cheap coffee table in front of him. Tassie sat at the other end of the couch, watching Luke play with his favorite wooden truck on the rug. The game was almost over.

"It's been a beautiful day in Los Angeles, folks," the announcer exclaimed. "And what a game! Under a minute left to play, San Diego 16, Raiders 14, first and 10 for the Raiders on their own 20-yard line."

"Come on, Raiders! Get your asses moving!" Hank bellowed as he popped open another beer.

"Back to pass, Plunkett's got good protection. It's a long one. Ohhh," the announcer groaned. "Just a bit too far. Wide receiver Montgomery couldn't get to the ball."

"What?" Hank roared. "That was pass interference if I ever saw it! Shit! Are you officials fucking blind?" He downed half his beer in one gulp.

"Up to the line of scrimmage, the snap. Plunkett back to pass, yes! Hits Parker, the tight end, for about 12 yards. No huddle, the clock's ticking, 37 seconds left to go, back again to pass—it's a blitz!—runs to his right, still looking. Nobody. Has to throw the ball away. The clock stops with 29 seconds left."

"Come on, Raiders! All you need's a field goal!"

"Raiders ball, second and 10 on their own 32."

"Okay, you woosies, field goal position coming up." Hank pounded the rest of the beer, crumpled the can and popped open another.

"Raiders up to the line of scrimmage. No timeouts left, Plunkett back to pass, nobody open, starts to his right, oh no! It's a sack! San Diego's middle linebacker came straight up the center. Plunkett sacked for a 10-yard loss."

"Goddamn it!" Hank shrieked. "Where the fuck's the protection?" He took another gulp of beer.

"Raiders up to the line of scrimmage, back to pass again, he's getting pressure, throws a long one—oh no! Intercepted by San Diego. Tackled on the San Diego 35."

Hank threw his half-empty can at the TV set. Beer sprayed everywhere, onto the screen, the wall behind the TV and the rug below. "What a bunch of pussies! Threw the goddamn game away!"

Tassie couldn't help herself. "Hank, look what you did! Christ! It's just a game."

"Shut up, Tassie! They played like a bunch of pussies." Hank snapped his fingers. "Luke!" Instantly, Luke dropped his toy truck, and rolled over onto his back. Wide-eyed, he held his arms and legs up in the air, like an obedient puppy, just as Hank had trained him to do.

Tassie jumped up from the couch. "Hank, stop that! Don't take it out on Luke!"

"Shut up, bitch!" Hank stood up, grabbed her shoulder and gave her a slap that sent her sprawling on the floor. "Don't you fucking ever tell me how to handle my son!" Hank stepped over Tassie, grabbed his gun from atop the refrigerator, and stalked out of the house.

Tassie waited until she heard Hank's car start down the gravel driveway. Luke stayed motionless on his back, hands in the air, knees drawn up toward his chin. He began to move his head slowly from side to side, arching his little neck, looking for his father, waiting for the command to become a human being again. Tassie crawled over to her baby. When she tried to pick him up, he squirmed and started to cry. "No, no, just Daddy."

Tassie picked him up and hugged him. "It's okay, it's okay, honey. Don't cry. Daddy's gone. Don't cry. Momma's going to take care of you. Don't you worry." *Yes. Don't you worry. Momma's going to take care of everything.*

Monday morning. Mother and daughter sat in a corner of Aunt Aggie's Tea Shop and Creamery. Luke lay sleeping in his stroller next to them. The sagging shelves on the shop's blond, knotty pine walls were laden with little porcelain kittens and puppies, round-eyed dolls, ornate picture frames, music boxes, miniature tea pots next to little packets of tea with names like "Indian Moonlight," tiny pillows embroidered with maxims such as "Home Is Where the Heart Is," and other assorted bits of kitsch. Tassie figured this was the last place Hank might find her or see her by accident. Even if he'd followed her, when he saw her mother, he wouldn't come in.

"Mom, I'm scared. Really scared. Hank's out of control. I'm afraid he could hurt me—and Luke."

Mrs. Daniels delicately sipped her tea. "Well now, dear, it can't be that bad. I've told you before, it's his job. Puts him under a lot of stress."

"And I've told you it's not his job. It's something else. And he's getting worse, much worse. Soon he's really gonna snap. And I don't want to be there when he does."

"Why do you say he's getting worse? Has he said or done anything different?"

Tassie stared at her mother, trying to decide how much to tell her. Finally: "Mom, I haven't told you much about Hank and our marriage. I didn't want to worry you and Dad."

"You won't worry us, Tassie. Please."

"I didn't tell you about the dog."

"You have a dog? We never saw it." Mrs. Daniels took another sip of tea, set the cup down firmly, and clasped her hands over her plump belly.

"I know you never saw it, but you've seen the tree."

"What tree?"

"The large oak growing in the field behind our house."

"Tassie, darling, you look so worried. What can be so frightening about a tree?"

"It's not the tree. It's Hank." Tassie nervously took a few sips of her lukewarm coffee. "Okay. The dog. Listen. One day last month, Hank came home for lunch. I didn't expect him. But he's always done that, pop up when I don't expect him. In the beginning, I thought it was romantic. Like he just wanted to see me."

"Wasn't that a good thing?"

Tassie's hand was trembling as she took another sip of coffee. "At first, yes. But then it changed. Now it's like he's always watching me."

Mrs. Daniels sighed. "Go on, Tassie. What about the dog?"

"Yes, the dog. That day Hank brought home a Doberman puppy he'd picked up from the Humane Society. He said it was a present for me, something to protect me when he wasn't around. Hank started to roughhouse with it in the kitchen. I guess the dog didn't like to be touched. It spun around and bit Hank on the hand. Not hard, it barely drew blood. But Hank went off like a bomb. He screamed at the dog, snapped on its leash, and yanked hard on its choke collar. Then he dragged the dog outside and tied it to the tree. Hank ran into the toolshed, cursing and screaming and came out with a chain. He started to whip the puppy with the chain. Hank didn't know I was watching him from the kitchen window. At first, the dog barked and jumped at Hank, but each time it was jerked back by its choke collar. Hank just kept screaming and whipping the dog.

Mrs. Daniels leaned forward, eyes wide. "Oh, my God."

"Finally, the dog stopped jumping. It just lay there whining. Hank kept whipping it, even after it didn't get up any more. I thought he would never stop. Just kept hitting it, and hitting it. The dog was bloody everywhere. I wanted to run out, try to stop Hank, his arm with the chain in his hand, rising and falling, over and over, the dog lying on the ground, whimpering. But I was afraid. I knew if I interfered, Hank would turn on me."

Mrs. Daniels looked at her daughter in disbelief. She reached out and grabbed Tassie's hand. "Oh, you poor darling. You should have told me then."

Tassie pulled her hand away. "What good would that have done?"

"I'm not sure. But I wish I'd known. Still, I don't understand about the tree."

"The tree. That's where he buried the dog. He got a shovel from the shed, dug a little grave, threw the dog in and covered it with dirt." Now Tassie couldn't stop talking. "Okay, you know about the dog and the tree. Every day since then, I've looked at that tree. And I see the dog, and I hear its howls."

"Honey, you've got to get away from this."

"I know, I know. And here's the really strange part. A couple days ago, Hank came home in the middle of the afternoon. He went to the shed and grabbed a hatchet. I watched him from the kitchen. He went to the tree, screamed, and hacked at it for a minute or so. He hardly dented the tree. He screamed again and threw the hatchet across the field as far as he could. Then he ran out of the yard, got back in his car and drove away.

"Tassie, he's crazy." Mrs. Daniels shuddered and took a hasty gulp of tea.

Tassie started to cry. "And yesterday—yesterday, he blew up at a football game on TV! He hit me. Knocked me down."

"He hit you?"

"Yes! And did you know Hank trained Luke to roll over on his back like a puppy on Hank's command?"

"Oh, the monster."

"He's not a monster. He's a man." Tassie crumpled her paper napkin into a tiny ball and dabbed her eyes. "When Hank came home later, he was all apologies. He even cried, and said how much he loved me. And part of me still loves him. Mom, the first night I kissed him, I felt he was the loneliest person I'd ever met. But he's keeping something inside. And I just can't get at it, can't make it better."

Mrs. Daniels slowly nodded her head. "Something in his past."

"Yes, something about the war. About the jungle. Even in his sleep, he can't forget."

Mrs. Daniels reached over and again took Tassie's hand. "You poor dear. Why did you ever marry him?"

"Because I loved him. I thought I could change things, I told you already. I was sure I could make everything all right."

"But you couldn't, could you."

"No. And now I think *I'm* going crazy, too. I think he's watching me every minute. I'm always afraid. And the slightest thing sets him off."

"Tassie, I wish you'd told me about this a long time ago. You've got to get away from him."

"I know."

"Can't you just leave? Take Luke and go somewhere?"

"Mom, Hank's a cop! The moment he even thinks I've left him and taken his son, he'll have every cop in the country looking for me. No. I need time—and distance. Somewhere he can't find me. A place where I'm not afraid."

"How can I help?"

"Just do exactly what I tell you. Will you?"

"Yes, of course. Anything."

"All right. First, I want you to call me tonight when Hank's at home. Invite me to go on a shopping trip tomorrow to San Francisco. Union Square. And I need to borrow some money. As much as possible. Bring it with you in cash."

Tuesday morning, Mrs. Daniels drove Tassie and Luke into the City. They parked in the Sutter-Stockton Garage and put Luke in a stroller. When they reached Union Square, Tassie stopped. "Mom, you take Luke with you to Macy's. I've got my own shopping to do."

"Why can't we all shop together?"

"I need to get some things for myself."

"What things, dear? Can't you find them at Macy's?"

"No, Mom. I can't."

Mrs. Daniels looked skeptically at her daughter. "Tassie, what are you up to?"

"Nothing, Mom."

"Of course you are. You can tell me."

"No, Mom, you don't need to know."

"You can't tell me anything?"

"No, I can't. I'll meet you back here for coffee in an hour."

"Well, what should I tell Hank if I see him? He's sure to ask."

"Tell him the truth—part of it. We went window-shopping and stopped at Macy's. Then we had coffee and pastry in Union Square. And that's all you tell him."

Mrs. Daniels compressed her lips in annoyance. "Oh, all right, Tassie. But I don't see the need for such secrecy."

"I do."

Mrs. Daniels took the stroller and pushed it slowly across the square toward Macy's. Tassie looked all around her carefully, then headed out Sutter toward Polk Street to do her shopping. All the way, she scanned the streets for any sign that she was being followed. Tassie really was beginning to wonder if she was becoming as crazy as Hank.

Wednesday evening. Time to put Luke to bed. Hank gave him a goodnight kiss on the cheek, and then handed him to Tassie. While she was bathing the boy, Hank popped his favorite bondage flick into the VCR, turned the volume on low, and slouched down on the couch. After the bath, Tassie put Luke in his bed, carefully covered him with a blanket, and returned to the living room. Quietly, she sat down on the couch next to Hank. A moment passed. He put his hand on her knee and slowly worked his way up her thigh to the groin. Helpless, seemingly drained of all energy, Tassie watched the movie, afraid to move. *Does he suspect anything? Could he have followed me in the City?* Very slowly, she took a deep breath. *You owe it to Luke. It's now or never, girl. You can't chicken out.*

Tassie blinked. *Time to move.* Her heart was pounding so hard she thought her ribs would break. Her hands were stiff, her fingers like icicles. *Go!* She forced herself to smile at Hank, stood up, and walked slowly into the kitchen. Hank continued to watch the movie.

Tassie looked at the gun that sat on top of the fridge, a few short steps away from Hank. She walked to the sink and carefully cleaned up the dinner dishes. *Remember, everything nice and normal.*

When she'd finished the dishes, she glanced quickly back toward the living room, then quietly took a package out of the cupboard where she'd hidden it. She slowly walked back into the living room past Hank and into the bathroom. Tassie began to take off her clothes. *This is it. Too late to quit now.* She took another deep breath, exhaled slowly, and continued undressing.

In the living room, Hank was glued to the show. He was watching his favorite scene where the woman was handcuffed in a sling and three men wearing black leather hoods were enjoying her in a variety of ways. Hank loved to see the woman wriggle in her bonds and hear her soft moans of apparent pleasure. Just as the scene ended, Tassie re-entered the living room and crossed quickly between Hank and the TV screen. She turned to face him. Hank's jaw dropped.

Little Tassie Bruner wore a studded leather collar around her neck, a leather bra with nipple holes, tight leather shorts open at the crotch, black fishnet stockings, and a pair of four-inch, red stiletto heels. Her arms were sheathed to the elbow in black latex gloves. In her right hand, she held a black velvet riding crop. "My turn tonight, honey," she purred. "Get out the cuffs."

Hank was in heaven. There she stood, his ideal woman. Kinky! Already aroused by the movie, Hank looked hungrily at Tassie. At last! She was really coming around to his point of view. Tassie nudged his chin with the riding crop and pointed to the bedroom. Quivering, Hank obeyed.

A soft *click*. Then *ping—click*. Steel on steel. Again *click, ping—click*. More steel. Silence. Then again, *click, ping—click. Click, ping—click*. Silence.

Hank Bruner lay naked on his back, spread-eagled across the sheets, securely cuffed to the heavy steel bedstead. The room was like a sauna. Tassie's black shadow moved sinuously through the pot jungle shadows on the wall opposite the heat lamp. She whacked her left hand a couple times with the riding crop. Like a hungry cat, she approached the bed and ran the tip of the velvet whip up and down Hank's now throbbing erection. "Beautiful, beautiful," he hoarsely whispered. Tassie slowly removed the stiletto heels and walked to the end of the bed. She leaned over and grasped Hank's legs above the knees. Slowly, she pulled herself onto the bed. Her breasts brushed his flesh as she crawled up Hank's body and straddled his torso.

She softly rubbed his taut belly with her crotch as she ran her gloved hands around his nipples. Suddenly, she rose to her knees, arched her back, and thrust her sex within inches of his face. "You want some of this, honey? Shall I come closer?" Hank could barely groan his assent. In slow motion, she brought her pelvis down and pressed it to Hank's lips. She closed her eyes. "Don't stop, don't stop," she whispered and pressed down harder.

In a few moments, still in slow motion, she withdrew herself from Hank's now bruised lips, leaned forward and began to lick his ears, his neck, his chest. Slowly she worked her way down his sweat-glistening body, then ran her tongue up the shaft of Hank's straining penis. She wanted him to sleep. When she took him into her mouth, Hank immediately exploded. "Oh, beautiful, beautiful!"

Tassie smiled as she slowly relaxed her body. "Shhh, shhh. Go to sleep, baby," she cooed. "Go to sleep."

When Hank began to snore, Tassie crept off the bed and went into the bathroom. She stripped off her costume, slipped back into her jeans and black cotton sweater, and tiptoed through the tropical bedroom into the hallway and down to Luke's room. Luke whimpered in his sleep as she picked him up and carefully wrapped him in his blanket.

Suddenly, Hank was wide-awake. Something was wrong. He felt it. Quickly, he looked around the room. "Tassie, where are you?" he shouted. "Tassie!"

Without a word, Tassie crossed the bedroom to the closet and yanked out the small suitcase she had packed the day before. "What are you doing?" Hank thundered. "Take these goddamn cuffs off me! Now!"

"Later, dear," she answered.

"Goddamn it! Take these cuffs off! You bitch! I'll kill you!" That's precisely what Tassie was afraid of. Hank strained his whole body and thrashed about on the sheets. The bed shook and shuddered on the floor. The cuffs cut into his wrists and ankles. He didn't feel the pain.

"Goodbye, Hank." And Tassie and Luke were gone.

Sweat. The air was heavy, steamy, dense with the smell of sweat mingled with a faint burning odor from the red-hot heat lamp placed on a wooden box and trained on Hank's precious pot plants. And fear. Hank writhed and shook and roared. He continued to curse and twist as the heat lamp toppled to the floor. The pot jungle shadows on the wall vanished. A red glow slowly suffused the room. "Goddamn it!

Tassie! Tassie!" The pungent smell of burning pot soon filled the house. The night wind sighed and rustled the tall grass in the meadow.

Tassie ran down the driveway clutching Luke. Freedom! The exhilaration of flight to safety. No more subjugation and bedtime bondage. No more doggy rolls on the floor for Luke. She figured Hank's fellow cops would look for him when he didn't show up for work in the morning. His buddies would get a good laugh when they rescued poor Hank from his pot-farm dungeon. *Trapped naked in his own cuffs.* Tassie giggled through her tears.

She threw the suitcase into the Jeep, and then strapped the boy in tightly. She knew where she was going. Drive to the San Francisco airport and park in the long-term parking lot. From the airport, she'd take a taxi back to Oakland and catch a bus heading east. When Hank found the car, it would take him time to check out all the flights. This would throw him off for a while. She'd buy bus tickets for Salt Lake, but get off in Reno, and catch another bus heading north toward Canada. Once across the border, she'd figure out what to do next.

Tassie ran around the jeep and hopped into the driver's seat. She slammed the door shut, fumbled with the keys, and twisted the ignition switch. The engine growled, then revved to life. Tassie jammed the gearshift lever into first, lurched out of the driveway, and raced down the road to the highway. A quick right turn and off she headed for the freeway. *From this moment on*, Tassie vowed, *no looking back*.

And she didn't. She never saw the flames.

FLY GIRL

Professor Philip Winters knocked gently on the ancient oak door of an apartment in Barcelona's *Barri Gòtic*. No answer. He gave a push, and the door creaked open. The room was dark. He glanced again at the apartment number: 406. This was the number Toni had given him.

The dim bulb hanging from the corridor's water-splotched ceiling cast a faint glow for only a few feet into the room. Philip heard the flutter of wings and the squawk of a bird—a parrot? Toni always liked animals. "Toni?" Suddenly, a small, furry creature shot past Philip's legs and scrabbled across the hardwood floor. A cat? A rat? "Toni, are you alright?"

"Close the door," she said.

Philip obeyed. The room was black. And silent. His

eyes began to adjust to the gloom. Then he saw her, huddled in a corner, knees drawn up to her chin, eyes wide, staring at him. "Toni?"

Toni stood up. She hadn't bothered to put on any clothes. "Philip, I love you." Slowly, she walked up to him and laced her arms around his neck. "I said I love you. Are you going to answer me this time?"

Philip had known Toni since they were juniors at Santa Monica High. They'd seen one another in art class and in the halls with groups of friends, but he was too shy to approach her. Then, one lunch break in the spring semester, Toni sat down next to Philip on a cafeteria bench. "I've got some sketches I'd like your opinion on," she said.

Philip turned his head and stared. Toni was the embodiment of beauty one usually encounters only in romance novels. Thick waves of jet-black hair cascaded over her shoulders and flowed down her slender back. Her dark, arched eyebrows framed the tops of her almond eyes, eyes that caused Philip to lose himself in never-ending depths of erotic mystery when he looked into them. Delicate ears, oval face, chiseled jaw, perfect bow-shaped upper lip, and pouting lower. All this, and so much more, only inches away from him. Toni edged closer, and her thigh pressed against Philip's.

"Would you like to take a look?" she asked.

Philip blinked. His entire focus was currently on the feeling of Toni's thigh comfortably nestled against his on the bench. "I'm not much of a critic," he replied, without moving his leg.

Toni handed him the sketchbook. "I don't need a formal critique. I just want some ideas for a portrait I'd like to work on while my parents are traveling next month."

Philip opened the book. To his surprise, the first sketch was of him. "When did you do this?"

"Just a quick scribble in art class."

Philip looked at the second sketch, then quickly paged through the rest of the book. Every drawing was of him.

Toni flashed him a mischievous grin. "Do any of them show promise? Would you sit for the portrait? My older sister's always out with her college friends, so you and I'd be undisturbed in the house."

"Well, what about … you know, your friend, the baseball hero?"

"I'm sick of listening to him and his buddies prattle about sports and internal-combustion engines. I've decided I prefer blond, hazel-eyed scholars."

Philip nodded in agreement. "Usually a better choice."

"So what do you think about the portrait?"

"I think it's an excellent idea."

"My parents' plane leaves at 10 a.m. Sunday morning," she whispered. "What are you doing Sunday afternoon?"

The portrait went well. Very well.

Toni had gotten the best genes of her Spanish mother and her Chinese father. Her attractiveness was enhanced by her language skills. Her father had spoken to her mainly in Mandarin, her mother mostly in Spanish, and Toni had grown up in L.A. She could comfortably talk to half the world's population.

One of Toni's endearing quirks—perhaps a carryover from Mandarin—was her frequent use of metaphor and euphemism. If she wanted something, she preferred indirect suggestion to direct request. And she had a vast array of poetic phrases at her command. Any traditionally taboo subject such as sex or death was treated with sublime tact. Penis became "little brother" or "little bird." Philip's favorite expression of hers for making love was "to feel the clouds and the rain." And rather than say her aged grandmother was worried about dying, Toni would sigh and say, "The sunset is charming, but she fears it's very near dusk." And instead of describing a high school enemy as a wanker, Toni would merely state, "He often consoles himself," or "He frequently visits the five sisters." But at times, she displayed a keen sense of English language irony and sarcasm.

After graduating with an A+ average, Toni signed on as a flight attendant for a major Spanish airline. Philip had wanted her to go to college. She'd be a sure thing for scholarships, with her outstanding average and her ethnic status. They'd argued for weeks before her departure. But Toni was adamant.

A gloomy Philip drove Toni to LAX to catch her flight to Madrid for training. They had coffee at an airport cafe. "You're sure I can't change your mind?" Philip asked.

Toni sighed. "I've told you—I want the real world as well as books. Why should I prolong my adolescence and waste my time fending off frat boys with beer on their breath? "

"I don't consider Cal Berkeley as an attempt to prolong my adolescence."

"I don't mean for you. A professor needs the Ph.D., so go for it. I'm only talking about myself. Why can't you understand that?"

"I *do* understand that."

"Then what's the problem?"

"I don't want you to leave me."

"I'm not leaving you. I'm always with you. But right now, I need to learn more about the world outside of school. I want to see the planet, especially Asia and Europe."

"So you think you need to find your so-called roots?"

"My *roots* are here in California, with you. And you shouldn't mock anyone who *is* searching for roots."

"I'm not mocking anyone or anything. I just can't stand the thought of losing you."

Toni leaned over and kissed Philip softly on the cheek. "Silly boy. You should know better. Could any two people be closer than we are? Do you really think anyone else could take your place?"

"I don't know. The world's filled with exciting men. You'll certainly have your pick."

"You think so little of me?"

"What do you mean by that?"

"You think I'm doing this to go chasing after men?"

"Well, what am I supposed to think?"

"I could have all the exciting men I want right here in California."

"Then why do you want to leave?"

Toni looked at her watch. "My flight will be boarding soon. I have to go." She grabbed her purse and stood up.

Philip seized her arm. "Wait. I'm sorry. That was mean. I shouldn't have said it."

"You shouldn't have *thought* it!"

"I can't help it. The idea of you with someone else just drives me crazy."

"Then stop thinking about it."

"Easy for you to say." Philip let go of her arm. "Look, Toni, I'm sorry. Please, don't be mad at me."

"My plane won't wait."

Philip went home angry and dejected. He knew further argument with Toni was futile. But he couldn't quell the fear that he was going to lose her.

Toni's father, a devotee of the Tao Te Ching, had counseled her to embrace the doctrine of nonattachment toward ephemeral things—in other words, everything. Life is given to us free of charge, but our only certainty is that someday it will be taken back. The best we can do is try to minimize the pain along the way. When things arise—good or bad—accept them. When they disappear, let them go. This was her father's mantra.

Her father's fatalism was reinforced by his family history. When the civil war in China ended in 1949, Chairman Mao launched a great land reform campaign. He decreed that at least one landlord in every village in China be eliminated. Her dad's grandparents had the misfortune of owning property in a small village to the west of Beijing. Shortly after Mao's enlightened policy statement, grandmother and grandfather were hacked to death in an early expression of power to the people. A few years later, his parents—whose error was their university education—were slaughtered in Mao's drive to eradicate counterrevolutionaries. Toni's dad had managed to escape into Hong Kong. After many years of hard work and a bit of good luck, he'd reached L.A.

Toni's mother had her own brand of fatalism. A virtual library of Spanish proverbs, she could address any situation with a nugget of traditional Spanish wisdom. In the face of adversity, she would simply give a philosophical sigh and murmur *a mal tiempo, buena cara*—accept a hardship with composure. Her favorite phrase was *a lo hecho, pecho*—what's done is done; face up to it. Of course, she'd passed on her time-tested knowledge to Toni.

Although Toni shared each parent's philosophy, she applied their teachings in her own way. In the days of the first portrait of Philip, she had given herself body and soul to him, and had felt him do the same. Philip was hers, and she was his. Their love was not ephemeral. And she would never let it go, even if she could. Yes, of course, life is a river, impossible to stem or to cling to. But some loves are fated, and they endure because they are part of the nonmaterial essence of Being. She believed this with all her heart. Contrary to Philip's fears, her separation from him wasn't abandonment. Yes, it was a hardship, but a necessity that just had to be faced up to. To Toni, their reunion was only a matter of time.

Philip plunged into his studies at Cal Berkeley, and dreamed of Toni. At first, they wrote to each other often. But over time, they settled into a once-a-month correspondence. Toni was comfortable with this arrangement; Philip wasn't.

Her letters were filled with descriptions of exotic

destinations, chatty anecdotes about various people she'd met, and tales of the antics of her airline colleagues. *Did I tell you about my friend Roxanne?* Toni wrote. *She recently joined the fabled mile-high club.* Philip was not amused when he read this. Naturally, he wondered if Toni was also a member of this prestigious group. In his mind, not a flight went by without many men's blood pressure skyrocketing as Toni walked toward them down the airplane's narrow aisle, or, for that matter, when she walked away from them. *She later discovered that part of her initiation fee was treatment for a nasty case of gonorrhea! Poor girl.* This revelation disturbed Philip even more.

Philip's letters were mainly discourses on books he'd read, or unflattering psychological profiles of some of his professors. He failed to mention his own occasional liaisons. And though such relationships usually ended amicably, they were brief and unfulfilling. He tried hard to free himself from Toni's subtle yet all-powerful allure, but she had quietly crept deep into his heart, and would not be dislodged. Wasn't it just possible that Toni felt the same about him? Philip's imagination wasn't generous enough to offer him this assurance.

As time went by, Toni did accept a few invitations, but not the hundreds that Philip imagined. She had a brief affair with a Chinese artist who lived in a miserable Beijing *hutong*, a collective dwelling in which one had to walk a half block to the sole communal toilet. She broke up with the artist at the opening of his first one-man show at a big gallery out in the 798 Art Zone, Beijing's trendy, new international art and culture district. Once a cluster of dismal, soot-blackened factories under that great aesthete and humanitarian, comrade Mao, 798 had recently turned into a western-style art enclave, complete with wine bars, coffee houses, restaurants, and gift shops staffed with English-speaking clerks. The current Chinese authorities tolerated the galleries, however decadent they perceived the art to be. Toni's artist friend went on to cultivate an avant-garde reputation, and an avant-garden of Beijing's art groupies. When things disappear, let them go. Toni wished him luck.

It took Philip only three years to finish his undergrad work. Toni came to watch him get his diploma. After the ceremony, they strolled hand in hand through the campus. Philip stopped in the middle of a small bridge over a swiftly running stream. He put his arms around Toni and kissed her. Toni gave him a warm smile. "I'm so proud of you. You looked so handsome in your cap and gown."

"Thanks. You know I did it for you. Worked my butt off to fast-track things."

"And congratulations on your new scholarship. A full ride to a Ph.D. and presto! Instant professor."

"It's probably not quite that simple. But thanks. And thanks for being here."

"You knew I wouldn't miss your graduation."

"I'm just so happy you're back. And now, with the money I make as a teaching assistant and whatever you can make—maybe as a translator—we'll at least be able to pay the rent."

Toni pulled away. "Why would I need work as a translator?"

"Don't look so surprised. You know you can't fly if you're living here in Berkeley."

"Berkeley? Wait … at the moment, I live in Madrid."

"Well, yeah, at the moment. But you've been flying for over three years. And now that I'm a grad student, I figured you'd come back."

"But Philip … I'm not quitting my job yet. Come on, we've talked about this. You know how I feel. I'm not ready to stop flying. Maybe a couple more years, I don't know."

"I know what you said before. But that was months ago. People *do* change their minds. A lot can happen in a few months."

"Philip, lets be realistic. We're both only 21, much too young to settle down, as they say. My mom always told me—"

"I know, I know, your mom. She's a walking repository of folk wisdom. Don't jump into marriage and kids, she said, 'til you're ready for it. Just because that's what happened to her is—"

"Stop that! Leave my mom out of this."

"You're the one who brought her up! Just because she wasn't careful—"

"I said leave her out of this. You criticize my mother for trusting in popular wisdom. Well, you could stand a good dose of that wisdom yourself."

"Oh, yeah? Are you going to give me a lesson in Spanish folk philosophy?"

"Ever heard the proverb *los celos son malos consejeros*?"

"It's not jealousy! I'm in love with you. And, by the way, I know some aphorisms myself. *Amor de lejos, amor de pendejos*—long distance love is for idiots."

"Is that really what you feel, Philip?"

He was silent for a time. "Maybe we're kidding ourselves. Maybe we're just afraid to let go."

"I'm not afraid. And I have no intention of letting you go. I love you. I always will."

"So easy to say."

"That doesn't make it false. And it's only easy to say to the right person. I've never said that to anyone but you. And I never will."

"Of course."

"Philip, what are you so afraid of?"

"I don't know. But when you're not with me ... I feel so lonely. Just so lonely."

"Oh, Philip, I wish you could understand my needs, not just your own."

They stood in silence on the bridge and watched the stream beneath them flow over the stones and swirl around the larger rocks. Finally, Philip spoke. "I'll try to be patient, if that will make you happy."

"Okay."

They continued to stare at the stream, side-by-side, inches apart. Philip wanted to put his arms around her. But he didn't.

Later, they had a very quiet dinner, and once again Philip drove Toni to the airport. They parted with a sad kiss, both alone in their own thoughts. Philip watched Toni go through security and disappear down the long corridor to the gate for her flight.

Philip's student years continued to crawl slowly by. As much as he enjoyed his studies in Spanish, French, and English literature, each passing moment increased his sense of the inevitable loss of Toni.

Toni kept on traveling the globe. In one letter, she mentioned her parents' divorce. Her father had moved to Canada, and her mother and sister were now somewhere on the East coast. Philip was greatly saddened when he lost touch with Toni's family. His own father had been killed in a car crash when Philip was five years old. His mother was diagnosed with lung cancer in the autumn of his junior year in college. She died six months later. After Toni's parents' divorce, he felt as if he had lost a second family.

Philip saw Toni several times a year. Whenever they were together, it was wonderful. But he couldn't escape the notion that she had the whole world of fascinating men throwing themselves at her feet. Of course she didn't want to come back to share his mundane life in Berkeley. How could she possibly stay interested in a grad student slogging his way through a Ph.D. in

Comparative Literature, thereby consigning himself to a life of genteel poverty?

One Friday afternoon before Philip's final semester of grad school at Berkeley, Toni called him. "Hi, Prof. How's life in the library?"

"Just great. I love writing my dissertation: *The Influence of Pierre Ronsard on the Poetic and Psychosexual Development of Edna St. Vincent Millay.* Catchy title, isn't it? Where are you?"

"I've got a layover in L.A. How about joining me for a weekend of hands-on research?" Four hours later, Philip was in Toni's hotel room in Malibu.

On Saturday morning, they lazily lounged in bed, sipping coffee. Toni was smoking, a recently acquired habit that Philip disapproved of. She set her coffee cup down on her bedside table and ran her fingers through her hair. "Philip, I've been thinking. Maybe soon I'll be ready for a change."

Philip was silent. Toni puffed on her cigarette, set it in the ashtray, and rolled over onto her stomach. She playfully licked his chest. He squirmed and protested that he was ticklish. Ever since Toni began flying, he was always quiet and a little distant from her after they made love.

"I've seen a lot of places and met a lot of people:

businessmen, scientists, lawyers, doctors—"

"So you keep telling me. Any teachers in this fascinating mix?"

"Only you, Philip."

"Of course," he muttered.

Toni knew Philip didn't like to hear about the people—especially the men—she'd met. But she figured that perhaps a little nudge to his jealousy might spark her desired reaction. Had Toni been fully aware that Philip's jealousy was as intense as his passion for her, she might have chosen a different approach. "I get phone calls all the time," Toni continued. "One doctor from Spain has been calling me for months." She looked up at Philip. "He says he wants to marry me."

Before Philip could respond to this statement—which sounded curiously like a question—Toni's cell phone rang. She sat up, fluffed the pillows behind her, and reached for it. She knew Philip was looking at her. "Hello? Why, Dr. Alvarez." She smiled at Philip. "Yes, yes, of course I'm thinking of you. You're in San Francisco? How nice. What am I doing now?" Toni laughed. "Oh, just sitting here in the kitchen filing my nails. I'm waiting for my roommate to get out of the bathroom so I can shower. She's such a slowpoke." Toni glanced at Philip and smiled again. "No, I don't think

I'm busy Sunday night. Okay, call me when you get to L.A. Be good. Bye-bye."

Toni put the phone down and gave a theatrical sigh. "Speak of the devil. The doctor says he's in love with me. He's got a big house in Madrid, drives a black Mercedes, and wears these beautiful Italian suits." Slowly, Toni turned her head and gazed at Philip. "What do you think I should do?"

Philip only frowned. Toni reached for her cigarette, lay back against the pillows, took a deep puff and slowly exhaled. She gave a little laugh. "I *said* he wants to marry me." Still no response. Toni watched the smoke drift slowly upward. She stubbed out her cigarette. "Philip, I'd really love it if you kissed me."

Philip's flight left LAX at five-thirty Sunday afternoon. He and Toni spent most of the weekend in bed. After the phone call from Dr. Alvarez, Toni and Philip's lovemaking had an unusual intensity. Perhaps the thrill of mutual treachery? In his own mind, Philip staked his claim to Toni, secretly telling the Spanish doctor to eat his heart out, that Toni was Philip's woman, that the medico would never know the reason for Toni's laughter on the phone, that she and Philip were sharing a delicious secret, that their love was the real love, and that anyone else in Toni's life was an insignificant creature to be deceived, mocked, and discarded—in short, that Philip was dominant.

Philip got to Berkeley in time to prepare for his Monday morning seminar on Cervantes. On the plane home, he'd attempted to sort out his feelings. Try as he might, he still couldn't make himself believe that he was the only man Toni loved. But this time, he was determined to burn through his jealousy. He convinced himself that he felt more pity for the doctor than love for Toni. *I'm through driving myself crazy by saying goodbye to her and sending her off into someone else's arms.* Philip was also disturbed to discover the duplicity and brutal competitiveness that he had allowed to flower in himself. And he suppressed the vague notion that he'd missed something important between himself and Toni.

Once back in his apartment, it took Philip a long time to focus on his teaching plans. He couldn't escape the memory of Toni's smiles and coy little lies during her phone call with the doctor. *Who's she snuggled next to whenever I call her?* Philip wondered. And he was surprised to see how much he disliked feeling complicit in Toni's lies, in her deliberate toying with the poor guy at the other end of the line.

Ten a.m., Monday. Philip looked forward to meeting the new students in his morning class. He was sure his feelings of jealousy over Toni would soon disappear. Although the thought of their times together caused a surge of desire in him, an almost cruel urge to possess her, the rest was emptiness. He wasn't sure what this change in him meant, but at least he could once again focus on his work.

It pleased Philip to see that most of his students were already there when he entered the classroom. He greeted them, took questions about the syllabus, and asked them each to give a brief personal history and a statement of their academic goals. A few minutes before the break, someone knocked softly on the door, and, nodding apologetically, entered the room. Philip glanced at his class list. "And you must be Miss Rawlins?"

"Yes, sir. Elise. I'm sorry I'm late." She brushed a lock of auburn hair off her face and looked around for a chair. A very buffed student in a tight black T-shirt promptly took his backpack off the chair beside him, and smiled at Elise. However, she took the remaining vacant spot on the opposite side of the table. Philip approved of this choice. It was a sign of independence.

"Welcome, Miss Rawlins. Perhaps you would introduce yourself to the class?"

"Yes. Thank you. My name's Elise. I'm an art major, and I'm sorry I'm late, but my plane got in at midnight last night, and I overslept this morning, and then I got lost. But it won't happen again." She looked around the class, and smiled.

Philip nodded, accepting her apology. "You got in late. From where?"

"Boston. I'm a transfer student from Boston University."

"And what's your purpose in taking this class?"

"I'm interested in Spanish art, and I want to get a broader understanding of Spanish culture."

"A good reason." Philip glanced at his watch. "Let's take a 10-minute break."

The students closed their notebooks and began to chat as they filed out of the room. The buffed fellow got up and did a slow, panther-like stretch, which emphasized the magnificent muscular structure of his upper body. Again, he smiled at Elise, but she gave no indication that she planned to get up soon. His smile remained as he proudly swaggered from the room. Neither Philip nor Elise appeared to notice his departure.

A month passed. Since Malibu, Philip had received only one chirpy postcard from Toni. *Hi, professor. Here in Tokyo, it's fun, but way too crowded and futuristic for a small town L.A. girl. Can't wait to get back to the relative calm of Madrid, and once again prowl the Prado. XXOO, Toni.* The Prado! It's more likely she'll be prowling the good doctor's majestic bedroom. Philip would never know the irony in his bitter prophecy.

A few days later, Philip replied by firing off a sullen note on an old black and white postcard featuring Anita Ekberg frolicking in the Fountain of Trevi. *Hi, Fly Girl. I'm having a great time here in the dustbin of scholarship, slaving over my critical works, and developing a fluorescent-light tan. Have fun in Madrid. Philip.*

A few hours after he mailed the postcard, Philip ran into Elise in a coffee shop near campus. She wore a turquoise cashmere sweater. Loose, yet pleasantly clinging, it revealed more than it pretended to obscure.

"Hi, Elise."

She looked up and gave him a warm smile. "Hi, Mr. Winters."

She stood up and extended her hand. Her handshake was firm. Philip couldn't help but admire her long legs, sheathed in black leggings and black suede ankle boots. "What are you reading?" he asked.

She held up the book. "*Meditations on Quixote* by Ortega y Gasset."

"Do you like it?"

"I guess so."

"Please, sit down. Do you mind if I join you?"

"Oh, no. Not at all. Please do."

The conversation quickly proceeded from literature to personal life and funny stories about their past. It continued through dinner, and ended when they reluctantly said goodnight at the door to her apartment. Toni's name never came up.

Within a few weeks, Philip was risking his teaching career by dating one of his students. He and Elise would meet at places they hoped we're sufficiently out of the way. The pair worked out a cover story in case they were spotted, but their luck held. If they were seen, nobody reported it to the administration. Toni had stopped writing. This puzzled Philip, and he mailed her an angry note reminding her of his existence. Several times, he tried to call her. He got no answer. This made him even angrier. The worst thing she could do was ignore him. What's going on? Was Malibu her way of saying goodbye? No doubt, she was now a hundred percent occupied with her wealthy Spanish paramour. The hell with her and her global stable of lovers.

Philip finished his dissertation, got his degree, and looked forward to the part-time teaching jobs he'd managed to line up for the fall. He and Elise celebrated by taking a weekend road trip to Monterey. They'd packed a lunch that they planned to enjoy on the beach near the Santa Cruz Boardwalk. As they entered Santa Cruz on coastal Highway 1 in Philip's vintage black Saab, he glanced over at Elise. "Elise? Am I wrong, or are those tears?"

Elise sniffed, and turned her head away. Philip was alarmed. "You've been so quiet the last few days, and now you're crying. What's wrong?"

"Nothing."

"Please, we both know that's not true. I've never seen you this way."

"It's alright, darling. I'm fine."

They drove on in silence until Philip turned off the

crowded street and headed toward the beach. "We'll stop for our picnic and you can tell me what's wrong."

"I'm not hungry."

"Well ... okay. We can just take a walk."

Dark clouds lumbered slowly across the sky as Philip parked on the street a few blocks from the ocean. He ushered Elise out of the car and locked the doors. A faded gray pickup truck with several surfboards resting in back cruised slowly past, radio blaring, bass thumping so loudly that the truck's sheet metal vibrated. Three guys with sunglasses and bill caps snuggly on backwards sat in the cab. One of them whistled at Elise. Philip put his arm around her shoulders. Slowly, careful to match her pace, Philip walked with her toward the water. They passed a high-rise hotel, and walked out on the municipal pier. The cries of seagulls mingled with the tacky carnival music from the amusement park that sprawled along the Boardwalk. The muted roar of the surf and the hiss of the water running up the sand were occasionally punctured by the high-pitched squeals of children tumbling off their boogie boards, and then clumsily lurching along in the cold, gray water near shore. The wind off the ocean carried the smell of salt and fish, though the fresh sea air was sometimes freighted with the foul odor of deep-fried food that came from the greasy smoke roiling through the ventilators of the ramshackle restaurants that lined the pier.

Suddenly, Elise stopped. "We don't have to keep it, you know."

Philip just nodded his head. His intuition had been confirmed. Quietly, he pulled her close as he found himself fighting back his own tears. "I figured that was the situation," he whispered. "But don't worry. Let's talk about it. Please understand. I'm not upset."

"Thank you for that lie, Mr. Winters." Elise put her head on his shoulder and let her tears flow. "I don't know how it happened. We've always been so careful," she sobbed.

Philip held her tight. "Shhh. Shhh. It's not the end of the world. Maybe it's a good thing."

Elise looked up at him. "You really think so? And please don't try to comfort me with another polite lie."

"I'm not lying. Do we love each other?"

"Yes. At least I love you."

"Then don't worry. We can work this out."

They walked to the end of the pier. Together they watched the waves roll slowly toward the shore.

Elise moved in with him soon after they returned from Monterey. Philip sent a wedding invitation to

Toni, but never got a response. Many months later, he received a wedding announcement from her. Yes. Of course. She was now the wealthy Señora Alvarez.

Try as he might, Philip couldn't forget Toni. He tormented himself with visions of her as an exotic jewel on the doctor's arm, a glittering Eurasian beauty who spoke *Castellano puro*, worldly, but by no means blasé. No doubt, her attractiveness was augmented by her sincere curiosity at dinner parties and gallery openings. For once, Philip's imagined scenario was largely accurate. And, as he angrily suspected, Señora Alvarez did continue to have her share of penthouse dinners for two in various world capitols, high above the blinking lights and human struggles below. Once again, however, Philip's imagination greatly exaggerated the number of such occasions.

Two years after their son was born, Philip and Elise had a daughter. Philip landed a tenure-track position at a small college north of San Francisco, and Elise worked on her M.A. Once both children were in pre-school, Elise became an art teacher at a local private high school.

Philip was happy. He was sure of it. He often thought about what made a long marriage successful. Certain factors contributed: a strong sexual attraction, mutual interests and values, respect for each other's character and actions, a shared sense of humor, each partner's equal capacity to love and be loved, open communication, mutual trust, love of family, and eventually a rich and rewarding shared history. And of course, there are all the little things like enjoying the same wines, liking the same kinds of music, and not watching TV news shows.

Philip and Elise looked forward to a lengthy history together. Their one recurring argument centered around Philip's desire to buy a pied-à-terre in Europe, a small condo would do, somewhere on the Mediterranean coast, perhaps in or near Barcelona. "Why would you buy something now? We can't afford it," Elise would say. Philip's counter argument was that a small apartment would be great for all of them and that prices were only going up. They could sometimes rent it out, and Philip was in Spain as a guest lecturer often enough to check on the place.

One day, Philip ran into Frank Janowitcz, an old high school friend. They had a cup of coffee together at the cafe Sorrento on Telegraph Avenue in Berkeley. As they sat down, Philip gave Frank a big grin, partially because he was glad to see him, and partially because he noted that Frank was becoming—as Frank would later describe himself—a "follicly challenged man of girth." In contrast, Philip still pursued the gentlemanly sport of fencing that he'd taken up in college. Swordplay plus jogging and an occasional workout in the gym had kept him fit. And Philip still had a full head of hair.

Frank was now a successful real estate broker who took an interest in both local and international property. "By the way, Philip," Frank enthused, "you'll never guess who I saw on the plane the last time I went to Madrid."

Philip realized, with a jolt, that he probably could guess, but he said no, he couldn't.

"Your high school girlfriend Toni. And boy, she's still a knockout." Frank moved his hands in a violin-shaped gesture as he spoke. "All that black hair, hanging down right to that sexy, round little—oh, sorry Phil. Anyway, she hasn't aged a day. And she asked about you."

A warning signal flashed through Philip. His stomach contracted. Stay away. You're happy. But by the time the signal reached his groin, the message was different.

"Oh? What did she say?" Images of his last meeting with Toni only one year earlier flashed through Philip's mind. They'd met by coincidence at JFK. She'd just arrived on a flight from Madrid, and he was in New York to attend an academic conference. Toni had insisted on buying him dinner at her hotel. She said she liked her life in Madrid, and asked how Philip's wife and kids were. After dinner, without a word, she had taken his hand and led him to the elevator and up to her room.

Philip had awakened early the next morning. He was miserable. What was he risking? His future? His wife's future? His children's future? He rolled over. Toni wasn't in bed. For a second, he was puzzled. Then he heard her moving about in the bathroom. The door was closed. Now what? How am I going to explain to Toni that I can't—

"Bastard! God damn your soul!" Toni's voice cut into Philip's chest like a red-hot razor. Who is she talking to? He glanced at Toni's bedside table. Her cell phone lay next to a condom box. Philip was about to call out to her when suddenly she emerged, an expression of diabolical anger on her face like he'd never seen before. When she saw he was awake, her lips morphed into a radiant smile. "Hi, handsome. Short night, wasn't it."

"Toni, I ... I heard your voice in the bathroom. Who were you talking to? Are you okay?"

"Of course, silly boy." She slipped into bed and began to kiss his neck.

But Philip was too alarmed by her curses and the bitterness in her voice to respond. "Toni. Please, stop."

"And waste time?"

She began to kiss his chest, his stomach—he grabbed her shoulders. "Toni. We've got to talk."

She stopped kissing him, and wriggled up, face-to-face. "No need for us to talk, my darling. I know what you're going to say."

"What?"

Toni sighed. "That we're both married now, and that we can't see each other anymore."

"Yes."

"Okay. I agree with you."

Philip felt a pang of disappointment. "Alright. Good. Well then, I ... guess this is goodbye."

Toni opened her eyes wide. Tears began to form. "Do you remember the first time we were together, the first time we felt the clouds and the rain?"

"Of course I do."

"Then give me a goodbye kiss," she whispered. "That's all I ask."

Philip left her room several hours later, barely in time to make his afternoon conference. As he closed the door,

Toni called out to him. "See you soon, lover."

Now, sitting next to Frank in the Cafe Sorrento, Toni's words created enticing little echoes in Philip's mind.

Frank looked worried. "Philip? Are you okay? You seem to be in a trance or something."

"Oh … sorry. I was just trying to remember when I last saw Toni. It was so long ago."

"Oh, yeah? Well, she seems pretty current about your affairs. I told her I hadn't seen you since high school. She said she was just wondering how you like your new job."

"What new job?"

"Something about your tenure track thing."

Philip was puzzled. When he'd seen Toni in New York last year, they hadn't discussed it.

Ah, yes, summer in Berkeley, mused Philip, as he sipped his cappuccino a couple months after he'd met Frank. The aphids were colonizing every tree, sending forth their viscous honeydew that rained upon the parked cars beneath. The sticky goo coated the glass and sheet metal most democratically. Mercedes and Lexus were equal to vintage VW Beetles. Each vehicle received its fair share from the pesticide-free, arboreal vegetation above.

Telegraph Avenue was crowded with runaway teenagers mixed with local kids learning about street life before going off to college in the fall. The kids slouched in groups on the sidewalk. Noses, tongues, eyebrows, lips, navels, and who knows where else were pierced and sported jewels or silver studs. The youthful bohemians passed cigarettes around as they listened to drugged-out folkniks with cheap guitars trying to channel Dylan or Baez. The cafes were sprinkled with bearded, latter-day Rasputins feverishly writing in battered notebooks. And the parking police were relentlessly prowling in their little meter buggies, handheld computers poised, ever primed to pounce on a lawbreaker's vehicle.

Philip was in a good mood. He had most of the summer free to work on his next book—oh yes, he'd long ago sworn he would publish, not perish—and Elise was teaching at a local summer art program.

Earlier that morning, the email he'd been waiting for had arrived. Attached was a signed contract for two weeks of guest lecturing and seminar teaching at a university in Barcelona.

Coincidently, another email, this one from Frank,

alerted Philip to an apartment for sale in La Barceloneta, an eighteenth century enclave on the Mediterranean shore in the old section of Barcelona. Philip emailed Frank that he would check it out in a couple weeks.

Frank immediately wrote back. "An inheritance from a rich uncle?"

"No," wrote Philip, "a guest teaching gig in Barcelona, set up for me by a friend. But don't count on any finder's fees. I told you how Elise feels. Also, I know the Spanish real estate laws are a lot different than ours."

"Don't worry, buddy. The seller is motivated, and I've got Catalan friends who can grease the wheels for you."

"Okay, Frank. Just for you, I'll look at the place."

Philip finished his coffee and ambled up Telegraph toward the Cal library. Time to get to work.

At dusk, Philip bundled his laptop into his carrying case, then strolled across campus and up Euclid Avenue toward the modest, brown-shingled cottage he and Elise rented. The soulful sounds of Patsy Cline singing *The Tennessee Waltz* drifted out of his open living room window. Such beautiful music, Philip thought.

Elise was in the kitchen talking to the kids, who were finishing their standard dinner of plain pasta, sliced apple, raw carrots, and celery. Two cups of chocolate yogurt for dessert were ready in the fridge.

The kids squealed their hellos when they heard the front door close, and Elise came out of the kitchen to greet Philip. He noticed that two candles were placed in the center of their small, dark-walnut dining room table, and that places for two had been set. Elise walked up to Philip, put her arms around his neck, and pressed against him. "I had a long day of summer school classes, so I'm a little tense," she murmured softly. "I was hoping that after the children are safely asleep, you could relax me a little." She cocked her head back, looked up at Philip and smiled.

"I'll see what I can do, darling," he answered, and kissed her on the lips.

"We're having chicken dijonnaise. Crepes Suzette for dessert. A bottle of Chardonnay is on ice."

"Hmmm. That's a lovely start to the evening." Philip kissed her again. They walked into the kitchen, his arm around her waist.

Philip sat and talked to the children while Elise took their empty plates over to the sink. "Are you ready for chocolate yogurt?" Philip asked his daughter.

"Yes, daddy."

Philip turned to his son whose nose was buried in a Pokémon book. "And you, big guy?"

"Of course," came the crisp reply, and the boy continued to read. Philip and Elise had already signed the lad up for a special class in social skills.

"Excellent," Philip proclaimed, and got up to get the kids their yogurt.

Elise continued the dinner prep while Philip jollied the kids through their dessert, and then took them both upstairs to their rooms and tucked them into bed. He sang a little lullaby to his daughter, kissed her on the forehead, and gently closed her bedroom door.

He crossed the hall to his son's room. "All books away, little toad," he said with a smile. Philip sat on the edge of the bed and pulled the covers up to the boy's chin.

"Are you going to tell me another old-fashioned fable tonight?" the boy asked.

"Yup. This one's called *The Fox and the Grapes*." Philip told him the story, kissed him on the forehead, and crept from the room.

Elise had lit the candles and changed the music from Patsy Cline to cool, instrumental jazz. The quiet music and flickering candlelight emphasized the calmness of the night, the peacefulness of the house once the kids were in bed.

Philip opened the Chardonnay and poured the wine while Elise served the dinner. They raised their glasses to each other in a silent toast of contentment.

Philip gave Elise a sympathetic smile. "So, darling, you said today was a long day."

"Nothing all that extraordinary. Just having to deal with the intellectually challenged element in the class that took art because they think it's an easy credit. I'm paid to be a teacher, not a cop."

Philip nodded. "I know what you're dealing with."

"I suppose I should be grateful for being an art teacher, not an English teacher. Every time I hear the word 'like' being nonsensically interjected—at least six or seven times in the average sentence—I truly want to scream."

Philip laughed. "It's the same in college classes. Like-speak, all-speak, up-speak. Perhaps we're just getting old."

Elise gave a wry grin. "They *do* seem to communicate, I guess."

Philip reached for the wine bottle. "More wine?"

"Certainly, Professor."

Philip sipped his wine and stared through the glass at

the candles. "I got an email from Frank today."

"Let me guess. He just happens to have access to some great little apartments on the Mediterranean coast."

"Well, yeah, he mentioned the idea."

"Darling, I know it's a dream of yours. It's a good dream. If only we could afford it. Maybe when the kids are older. But then we'll be paying for college, of course."

"Of course." Philip continued to stare at the candles.

Elise reached across the table and took Philip's hand. "I'm sorry. I'm not trying to be bitchy. I just can't help thinking about the practical side. Is that okay?"

Philip sighed. "Of course, it's okay. It's a good thing one of us thinks about such things."

Elise stood up, came around the table, and put her hands lightly on his shoulders. "Shall we have the crepes now? Or, perhaps, later?"

I cannot rest from travel: I will drink / Life to the lees. Fine ringing phrases, thought Philip, for Tennyson's dauntless traveler Ulysses. But they ring hollow if you're alone at midnight in a foreign city, thousands of miles from home and family. Even if you're sipping sherry in the Opera Café on a warm Saturday night in Barcelona after attending a performance of *Carmen*. Philip was lonely. His loneliness increased as he observed the crowded cafe filled with people talking, laughing, drinking, and dreaming.

He had one more lecture at the University to give on Monday, followed by an appointment in La Barceloneta to view the apartment. Of course, he had no intention of buying it. Elise was right. Their budget would be stretched too thin. Why are some dreams always just out of reach? Philip ordered another sherry. He hated the thought of returning to his lonely hotel room. It had never occurred to Philip that Toni might also have spent countless nights in charmless hotel rooms feeling just as lonely, perhaps more so. Nor had he envisioned how often she'd ended a social evening by thanking her host, and catching a cab to return alone to her hotel.

Outside the Opera Café, the streets were still teeming with people. Philip knew that when he left the cafe, he would wander aimlessly for several hours just to distract himself from his loneliness, to tire himself out so he could tumble into the hard bed and sleep. He figured he'd head back to his room only after Las Ramblas emptied of tourists, and the brigade of old women emerged with buckets of water and mops to clean the pavement in preparation for the renewed onslaught of tourists at sunrise.

The clatter of dishes, the music on the sound system, and the shouts of the waiters almost drowned out the ringing of Philip's cell phone. Elise? Philip didn't recognize the number. Possibly someone from the University or something about the apartment? It's a little late for a business call, even in Spain. Covering one ear against the noise, he took the call.

"Hello?"

"Hello, professor. Long time, no see."

Philip left the Opera Café, his mournful solitude erased by a flood of conflicting desires. He wove his way through the flow of people on Las Ramblas, then turned onto Calle la Boqueria and headed into the oldest part of Barcelona, a tangled mass of cobbled streets and passageways known as the *Barri Gòtic*, the Gothic quarter. This crowded jumble of churches, government buildings, apartments, monuments, alleyways, hostels, restaurants, bars, and nightclubs sits on top of the twenty-three centuries of history that have buried the ancient Roman city of Barsino. The address Toni gave him was below Calle Jaume on a narrow passageway off the Plaza de Sant Just, an unadorned slab of yellowish-brown concrete, stinking of urine, butted up against the surrounding buildings' stone walls that displayed the patina of a thousand anonymous stains that had seeped into the porous stones over the centuries. The narrow alleyways that spin off Sant Just are lined with tall apartment buildings that block the sunlight. Claustrophobic in daylight, the area is a seemingly impenetrable black maze at night. Coming from Calle Jaume, she'd said, head for the alleyway straight across the square. Go into the alley. My building's the third one on the right. There's a tiny light above the code box in the entryway.

Philip crossed the square, entered the dark passage, and almost stumbled over the cluster of parked motor scooters that clogged the way. He found the doorway, and keyed in the four-digit code she'd given him. The latch clicked open. The foyer smelled like the damp basement of a tobacco warehouse. The tiny bulb that flicked on above him lit his way almost to the stairs. What's Toni doing in this dismal building in Barcelona? Why isn't she in her palace in Madrid, cuddled next to her rich husband? And how did she know I was here?

The bird squawked again in the dark. Philip stood still, agitated, confused, once again holding Toni in his arms.

"Philip. Can't you answer me? I'm telling you that I love you."

"How did you get my cell phone number?"

"Easily."

An annoying habit of hers, thought Philip. To respond to a question in a way that answers it, but obviously doesn't. "Toni."

"Okay. Friend of a friend."

Another evasion. Drop the subject. "Whose room is this?"

"Mine. I live here."

"What happened to the mansion in Madrid?"

"Dr. Alvarez and the new Señora Alvarez live there."

Philip wasn't sure what to make of this news. "Can we turn on the lights?"

"Sure thing, Professor."

Toni unlaced her arms from around his neck and padded quietly over to a mattress on the floor. She knelt down and switched on a small red-shaded lamp. Philip was surprised to see that the walls were covered with large paintings, each one a surreal blend of entwined lovers, often beneath or near a twisted cross with a faceless figure nailed to it. The matrix for every painting was a gigantic visage, a soft-focus face that filled the frame, and seemed to be watching both the figures in the painting and the viewer. The face was the landscape itself, merging background and foreground, an eerie, omnipresent spirit, looming out of the canvas, filtering into the room. Philip recognized the ghostly face; it was his own. "You painted these?"

"You forgot I like to paint?"

"I seem to recognize some elements of your work." Toni just smiled and shrugged. "But the crosses," said Philip. "I didn't know you were religious."

"I'm not," she said, with sudden bitterness. She took a deep breath, and settled herself Buddha-like, on the mattress. "Please come here, Philip. I need you near me."

Philip stared at Toni. He knew what would happen if he sat down. And suddenly, he didn't care. For years he'd tried to ignore, to forget, to finally expunge the passion he felt for Toni. He loved Elise, he loved his children, and he would never leave his family. But his desire for Toni—admit it, he told himself, his *love* for her—came surging back, amplified by years of suppression. He had a few more days in Barcelona, and he knew he wanted to spend that time with Toni.

To acknowledge and accept his feelings for her gave him a sense of exhilaration, of vitality, of freedom. He was surprised to see that he felt only a little bit guilty. After all, as Frank once told him with a wink, guilt is just another name for fear of getting caught. Sure, he wouldn't get caught, but that wasn't the point. He wanted Toni. He wanted time with the fascinating and strangely sad woman she seemed to have become. He wasn't going to throw this chance away. He crossed to her and extended his hand. With uncharacteristic meekness, she put her hand in his, and gently drew him down beside her. He softly kissed her forehead. She closed her eyes and tilted her head back.

According to the old alarm clock on the floor next to the mattress, it was midmorning when Philip and Toni awoke. They slipped on their clothes. The bird screeched and the cat ignored them as they headed out for breakfast. They strolled over to Las Ramblas and headed up toward the Café Zürich on Plaza Cataluña. Philip felt alive in every cell, fascinated by the surrounding kaleidoscope of moving humanity. All his senses were sharpened. The smells, the noise, the sights—all in a jumble—flooded into Philip's mind.

Las Ramblas: a ribbon of concrete teeming with tourists milling about like schools of fish. Thousands of competing body odors mingled with clouds of exhaust fumes from swarms of motorcycles weaving between the ruthless taxis that prowled the flanks of the central promenade. The air was filled with the cries of caged birds. Dogs were pissing on trees while their owners clustered and chatted. Portable flower stands overflowed with myriad shades of red, orange, and pink ivy geraniums. Women wearing clinging, black Lycra shorts pushed high-tech baby carriages. Human statues painted gold and silver stood motionless while hundreds of gawking bystanders bulged across the promenade, waiting to spot some movement, perhaps a wink when someone tossed a coin into the bucket in front of the pedestal. Restaurants everywhere, tapas and cañas, ice buckets filled with bottles of rosé, *cava* or white wine, La Boqueria market packed with people like vertical bunches of asparagus in a bath of sunscreen and sweat, the clatter of dishes and ten thousand cups of café con leche, constant chatter—"*la cuenta, por favor*," "*gracias*," "*a usted*,"—and everywhere printed signs in English urging everyone to beware of pickpockets. Homeless men in rags lay coiled asleep on grimy cardboard slabs tucked into doorways. Bunches of school children shrieked happily and darted among the swarm of adults. Church bells tolled amidst the tin chatter of automobile horns. Buses exhaled billows of dark, greasy fumes. The steady thump thump thump

thump of a computer bass poured out of the bars. Life-size photos of torrid flamenco dancers in dramatic reds were posted on theater walls and cafe windows. A combination of Bosch and Bruegel, Philip thought, the grotesque mingled with exuberant humanity. He felt wildly happy. But what about his family? He loved his wife. Why did that phrase sound so banal? He impulsively grabbed Toni's hand.

Miraculously, they found an open table at the Café Zürich. They sat down on the uncomfortable aluminum chairs, ordered café con leche and croissants, and watched the stream of people flow by.

"So, no more mansion in Madrid?"

"No. All gone."

"Do you miss it?"

"What do you think?"

"I guess you don't. What happened?"

Toni took a long time to answer. "He got tired of me ... rather quickly. After our marriage. Okay, I could deal with that. Besides, I admit I could never give him my best."

"Why not?"

"Stop playing games. You know why. It's your fault."

"Oh."

"Of course, he always had other women. That too, I

could deal with. After all, I was flying all over the world, not caged up in some nunnery. I had companionship. And, to tell the truth, I was sick of just being some rich guy's wife. I wanted back to reality, the struggle, the ... oh, call it what you will."

"If you were so free, why bother with a divorce?"

Again, Toni hesitated. "He began to ... humiliate me. Like I was a servant. The first time, he asked me to make dinner for the two of us, then he brought another woman home and casually said let's all share. Then he did it again, and again. He insisted that I serve him and his women, pour their wine, and clear their plates. When they left, he'd wave and blow me a kiss. Say he'd see me the next day."

"So it was the doctor you were cursing that morning in New York?"

Toni took a gulp of coffee. "Who else? So, I snipped him."

"Pardon?"

"I snipped him! Not him, really, just his silk ties. Snip, snip, snip. Into the sink the pieces go. Next, his fine Italian suits. Snip, rip, snip. All over the bathroom floor and into the tub they fly." Toni began to cry. "And then his precious art collection. Stab, rip, snip. The fragments of his lovely paintings flutter to the floor, like dying butterflies. Then, I walked out the door, and never went back. Simple as that. I signed the papers his lawyers sent me, and, in a while, we were divorced."

Philip was extremely alarmed at the way Toni ended her marriage, and at the acid way she described it. But her tears moved him. He wanted to comfort her, but now he was afraid of the deep bitterness residing in her, something he'd witnessed a flash of once before in New York. All divorces are difficult, but her response seemed extreme. So what happens to her when I leave here? he thought. I can't lie to her. She knows I'm not free. What does she expect, and what can I give her? "So you—."

"I don't want to talk about it anymore," she snapped, and angrily brushed away her tears.

Philip reached for his coffee. "Of course. I understand."

"Don't you ever wonder what Elise is doing when you're away?" Toni had never spoken her name to Philip before.

"Not really."

"You're here with me. How do you know where she is?"

"Right now, she's probably home, asleep."

"So call her."

"Be serious. It's noon here, which means 3 a.m. in Berkeley."

"All the more reason."

"Don't be silly. I said it's the middle of the night there."

"I know that."

"Alright, I will." Philip called his home phone, and waited. In a moment, he glanced up at Toni. *After the tone, please leave a message.* "Hi, darling. I guess you must be sound asleep. Thought I'd call you before I got caught up in my lecture. I'll be in and out the next couple days—maybe even catch a late night flamenco show. How are the kids? I miss you." Philip hung up.

Toni was watching the people pass by, avoiding Philip's eyes. She took a sip of coffee. "So. She's not at home."

Philip bit off the end of his croissant and chewed it slowly. "Well, she's a very sound sleeper."

"No doubt there's a good explanation."

Philip ate the rest of his croissant. "I'll call her again. After I've seen the place in La Barceloneta."

"Good idea."

"Yes. That's what I'll do."

Toni finished her coffee. "Want to see the weirdest museum in the world?"

"Do I have a choice?"

"What do you know about crucifixion?"

Philip blinked. Once again. Typical non-answer. "What makes you ask me that?"

"I gather it's a very painful way to die." Toni gave a little laugh. "It's such a common symbol in Western culture, but it's been sanitized. Like a warm piece of beef, fresh-cut, dripping blood, that's then plastic-wrapped and put in a cold display case. It's no longer part of a once living animal, but rather a neatly packaged piece of protein that you can grill over a hot flame and enjoy for dinner, perhaps commenting on how tender the flesh is." Toni stood up. "Shall we go?"

Philip put some coins on the table, and they threaded their way through the crowd on the sidewalk past a very loud Dixieland jazz band that had just started playing in front of the cafe. Toni took Philip's hand. The light changed. They joined the mob that flowed across the street.

"One day, I discovered this museum tucked away near the cathedral. I found the image. You see, that's what he was doing to me. Crucifying me, mentally."

What was it that made Philip wonder if she was lying? "You told me. I'm sorry."

"So I studied the process of being crucified."

"Why did you stay with him so long?"

Abruptly, Toni stopped in front of a large, circular

fountain and let go of Philip's hand. "Why did you get married so soon after I saw you in Malibu?"

"Why? Well, if you remember, you stopped writing me. Obviously, you were totally involved with your Spanish doctor, and who knows how many others. You made that very clear to me. What chance did I stand, the proverbial harmless drudge?"

"I only got married *after* you married Elise," Toni said angrily. She looked at Philip and slowly shook her head. "You couldn't tell? The way we were together in Malibu. Such a beautiful flower in our bouquet. You couldn't tell? That weekend should have shown you how much we loved each other. Didn't you understand that?"

"No. I didn't. I knew how much I felt for you, but I was angry that you were seeing your medical friend. And only a few hours after I left!"

They stared at the fountain, watching the gushers of water struggling to reach up ever higher in the air. A puff of wind bathed them both in a fine spray. Toni welcomed the droplets as a cooling caress in the implacable Spanish sunlight. "Well, anyway," she muttered, "one can't repair the past." *A lo hecho, pecho.* But Toni also believed a corollary to this terse admonition: *A mala suerte, envidar fuerte*—loosely translated as "if misfortune strikes, raise the ante" or "never give up in a struggle." Toni had no intention of giving up. She reached again for Philip's hand.

They left the fountain, crossed another street, and strolled down the pedestrian Avinguda Portal de l'Angel toward the Cathedral. The peevish sounds of taxi horns and the wheezes of air-conditioned tour buses began to fade. Toni's hand felt soft and warm. Philip remembered the touch of her slender fingers as they'd slowly roamed his body the night before.

"So, as I was saying, the process of crucifixion is really horrible."

"Good grief. Are you still on that kick?"

Toni appeared to not hear the question. "It's slow, agonizing—excruciating in fact." She smiled at her little joke. "They nail you through the wrists or the hands to the horizontal beam, then bend your legs and nail your feet to the vertical."

"Toni. Stop. I really don't need to know all this."

"Sometimes they would break the victim's legs first."

Suddenly, Philip wasn't sure if he should comfort a wounded bird or flee from a dangerous madwoman.

"Poor boy," Toni said. "I know what you're thinking. Don't worry, I'm perfectly sane. I exorcise my demons through visual images, that's all."

They veered left on the Calle Dells Arcs, and eventually reached the Cathedral. Its Neo-Gothic façade gleamed down on the broad plaza.

"Ah, yes," Toni exclaimed. "The famous Cathedral of the Holy Cross and Santa Eulalia. Do you know about Santa Eulalia?"

"No," Philip replied.

"As usual, it's a story of men victimizing women. Eulalia was a Christian virgin—that's critical, the virgin part, of course—who at age thirteen refused to recant her Christian beliefs. To demonstrate her theological error, the clever Romans subjected the little girl to thirteen tortures. Three of them spring to mind. They put her in a barrel with knives stuck in it and rolled it down a street. They cut off her breasts. And they crucified her on an x-shaped cross. Eventually, Roman kindness won out, and they cut off her head. Now, she's the co-patron saint of Barcelona. What's left of her body is preserved in the crypt of the Cathedral. And you know what? Another gracious tribute to her memory is the flock of thirteen geese that live in the cloister's central courtyard. Imagine. One honking, shitting, pea-brained goose for each torture and for each year of the poor girl's life. But I suppose, since the geese are birds, they do sort of fit in the story, because a dove flew out of Eulalia's neck once her head was no longer in the way."

Philip stopped. "Toni, what's happened to you?"

Toni appeared to dismiss the question. "I've never seen the famous geese. But I'm told they're a popular tourist attraction. We're almost at the museum. Are you ready?"

"Ready for what?"

"You'll see." Toni led him through a tiny cobblestone alleyway on the eastern side of the Cathedral. They entered an ancient stone building, and passed through a square courtyard dotted with slender palm trees and surrounded by a brown stone arcade. The entrance hall of the museum was dimly lit by slits of windows set just below the dark, wooden ceiling. All traffic noise, exhaust fumes, shouts, laughter, the entire cacophony of the city was extinguished. The pair found themselves in a hushed crypt where time didn't seem to exist. The room was empty, but for a young woman—a pre-Raphaelite beauty dressed in a flowing crimson gown—at the reception desk. Without a word, the woman handed Philip and Toni their tickets, and pointed them toward the exhibit rooms. Philip was certain that he and Toni were the only visitors in the building.

The first room was even darker than the reception

area. Sickly white walls were barely illuminated by the tiny bulbs in black sconces affixed a few feet off the floor. In the center of the room stood a tall wooden cross with a life-size figure nailed to it. The sculptor who had carved the body of Jesus had paid attention to detail. Gouts of blood appeared to be dripping down the face from the crown of thorns. More blood poured from the deep, red gash in Christ's side, and uneven scarlet patches surrounded the iron nails in the hands and feet. On each wall hung another large cross with a life-size figure nailed to it. Every twisted body spoke of unbearable pain.

An old woman wearing an ankle-length black robe emerged from the doorway to the following room. Her garment rustled faintly as she drifted toward the couple. She raised her arm and pointed to the central cross. "Twelfth century," she rasped. Philip could still smell her stale breath as she gestured the two of them to proceed to the next room.

Once again, a tomb-like chamber, filled with life-size crucifixes. The old woman stood in the doorway, watching the couple, suspicious, guarding the crosses against the sacrilege of touching or sneaking forbidden photographs.

Philip and Toni entered the third room. Two crosses

stood back to back in the center, and on each wall hung two more life-size crucifixes. An ancient man wearing a black suit, white shirt, black tie, black shoes, with a black patch over his left eye limped up to them. The man stopped, gave a snaggletoothed grin, but said nothing. As the couple moved about the room, he followed them closely, and into the fourth room. Philip was starting to suffocate. "Toni, you came here all alone?" he whispered. "More than once?"

"Yes, I told you, it was therapeutic. It put my problems in perspective."

Was she being flip? Philip wondered. No, he decided. She was serious. They began to move more quickly. Room after room of petrified agony. Philip, almost desperate now, began to look for an exit. "Toni, let's get out of here."

In the next room, a green neon exit sign on the wall had an arrow that pointed upstairs. Philip wondered if this were some kind of maze. You have to go upstairs to get out? The worn wooden steps creaked as the couple climbed. The rooms upstairs were brighter, but the exhibits were the same. Philip and Toni followed more arrows on the floor, finally discovered one pointing down a stairwell, descended, and found themselves back in the reception area. The place was still empty of other visitors.

"I was beginning to hyperventilate," said Philip, as they crossed through the courtyard and exited the building.

"Pretty powerful, isn't it."

"Yes. Let's get a beer."

They found a quiet cafe near the Cathedral Santa Maria del Pi. "*Dos cañas*," Philip ordered. His nerves were jangled by the concentrated terror displayed in the museum, and even more by the depth of Toni's pain and anger. It can't be all about the divorce, he thought. It's just too much. They sipped their beer in silence. Finally, Philip sighed. "You've had a pretty bad time, I guess. A lot worse than I imagined."

"Not so bad."

"I can't believe that, Toni. Not after what you've told me and the bitterness in your voice."

"Stop! I don't want to talk about it," she spat. Then she looked at Philip and smiled. "Besides, you still haven't answered me, Philip. I said I love you. Are you afraid to say it? Or is it … is it that you just don't feel it?"

"Of course, I feel it. I'm just confused. I'm not sure if I can love two women at the same time."

Toni closed her eyes. Her whole body seemed to

relax. "So. You really do love me," she murmured.

Philip nodded. "I've got one more class in the morning. Then I stop in La Barceloneta. Let's have lunch tomorrow at the Zürich."

"You're not coming back with me tonight?"

"I want to. You know that. But I have trouble thinking straight when I'm around you. I'll meet you tomorrow, one o'clock, at the Zürich."

Early Monday afternoon, head down, shoulders hunched, Toni walked slowly up Las Ramblas toward Plaza Cataluña. Her eyes were puffy from lack of sleep, and caked with the residue of tears she'd shed as she lay alone through the dark hours, waiting for the sunrise and Philip. Toni's lessons in the real world had taught her that this globe is an exciting, lonely, beautiful, surprising, and dangerous place. Just *how* dangerous she'd found it to be, Philip would never know.

Toni's thoughts drifted back to the day on the cafeteria bench, the closeness she'd felt to that sweet, shy boy as she made her feelings an open book by the touch of her leg against his. And how she'd had to coax him to kiss her that first Sunday afternoon. And after that, how many tries it had taken her to finish the portrait during the month her parents were gone. She could see herself and Philip enter her house, day after day, and stare at each other 'til they burst out laughing. "Later!" they would shout together. "Life first. Art second!" And how her older sister had found the two of them, asleep in each other's arms, nude on the fireplace rug at three a.m. on the morning Toni's parents were due home. And how inseparable she and Philip had been from that month on until after high school graduation, when she had to leave—she had to—even if it meant stretching the connection with Philip, a connection she knew could never be broken. They'd have so much more to offer each other when they joined together again, forever. Soon, she had figured, Philip would attain his dream, Professor P. Winters, and look forward to a life of intellectual adventure. By then, she would have satisfied her need to see the world. She and Philip would spend summers in Provence, and university breaks in Paris or perhaps skiing in the Japanese Alps—just Philip and Toni together, as life had ordained. And as time went on, they would have a boy and a girl, and the cycle of life would continue.

How could he not know this? she wondered. After I told him everything, after I showed him how I felt when

I hung up after the doctor's call. Philip, how could you be so smart and yet so blind—so cruel! The clouds and the rain. So beautiful.

At Plaza Cataluña, Toni automatically joined the flow of pedestrians crossing the street toward the outdoor tables at the Zürich. As usual, she was blessed with good table karma. She slumped down at a prime spot in the shade just as a duo of German tourists stood up and walked away. She ordered a coffee, and waited for Philip. Don't get any false hopes up, she told herself. He's going to arrive with his goddam sanctimonious conventional guilt trip and tell me the same old story. And off you'll go, Toni. Spinning back into the cosmic garbage bin. She grabbed a napkin, brushed away her tears, and stared at her coffee cup.

It's true; you can't repair the past, she thought. But if there's one thing I could never take, it would be Philip's pity. Never knowing if he just feels sorry for me. I was lucky, the surgeon said, not to have permanent brain damage. Sorry, Philip, I lied. But my lie was for your own good. And for mine. Let him think I hate my ex-husband. Philip will never know the truth.

A jumble of memories flooded her mind. I woke up after the attack, and there was Dr. Alvarez on a metal chair at the foot of my bed. He stood up so fast the chair tipped over. *Agradezca a Dios*, you're alive! Can you talk? I laughed. Dr. Alvarez, I said. He took my hand and kissed it. Five months, he told me. Five months in a coma. Then, pop! Out I came. Other doctors and nurses were suddenly there. Keep calm, dear, the older nurse said. Don't excite yourself too soon. I came to see you everyday, said Dr. Alvarez. There are still things I can't remember, I told him. It was misty, late at night. I was walking alone through a dark plaza, something ... someone grabbed me, the smell of beer and onions, I screamed, I screamed—Shhh, shhh. Dr. Alvarez put his hand on my forehead. Don't think about it now. Don't try to remember. Look at the sunlight. The people around you, today. You're going to be okay.

You weren't raped, the nurses told me later. Your attacker must have thought you were dead. Be thankful for small favors, I said. Then one day, I was out of the hospital and back at the Alvarez home in Madrid. He gave me my own room, and took care of me. He also gave me a large white cotton bag, a laundry bag of mail. I had your mail forwarded to me, he said. I knew you'd be okay. You have many months' worth of letters. Don't worry about anything. I opened the bills and paid them, he said.

I went through my mail. That's when the real nightmare started. And the hate. The burning, gnawing, blinding hate for the man—the beast—who stole you from me, Philip. I fought hard in the dark, and screamed, screamed—suddenly there was nothing. God damn his soul! The faceless monster that attacked me. The nurses told me I'd been hit on the head with a heavy object. Yes, the real nightmare, Philip, began with your letter—not a letter—an invitation. A formal invitation, printed on a piece of fine white linen cardstock, so stiff, so impersonal. An invitation to your wedding. Mr. and Mrs. H. T. Rawlins request the pleasure of your company at the wedding of their daughter Elise to Philip Winters, to be held on blah, blah, blah. That man, that creature who stole you from me, you will never know that it's *him* that I hate. He's the one on the cross. You will never know. Don't cry, Toni. Whatever scrap of Philip remains for you, at least it's real.

A mime was performing on the sidewalk for the Zürich patrons. His shtick was to carefully observe the passersby, quickly fall in step directly behind an unaware victim, and do an exaggerated imitation of their walk: hippo stomp, gazelle light-foot, nervous rabbit, cape buffalo swagger, menacing tiger prowl—all reduced to absurd comedy.

Toni glanced to her right and spotted Philip emerging from the metro entrance. She watched as he crossed the street with the crowd, and worked his way over to her table. He waved to the waiter, and sat down. He was obviously excited, or was he just tense?

Toni met his eyes. "So. What happened?"

"I did it. I bought it."

"You bought the condo."

"Yes."

"That's wonderful," she breathed. Toni stared at her coffee cup. She picked it up carefully, took a sip, and slowly set it back on the table. She rested her hand lightly on Philip's knee. "Only one final thing to do," she murmured. "Tell Elise the good news."

"Now? Remember, it's the middle of the night in California."

"Now."

Toni's hand remained on Philip's knee. He took out his phone and called home. It rang several times before Elise answered. "Elise? Hi, it's me. Did I wake you? How are the kids? ... Great. What am I doing? Just having a coffee at the Zürich. Yes, of course, I'm thinking of you." Philip glanced at Toni. "What? I sound excited? Well, actually, I am. Guess what? I bought the condo.

It's perfect. Yes. I know ... I know, but I got a really good deal." He looked again at Toni. "Elise, I need to stay here an extra week or so to handle the details. Believe me. When you see the place, you're going to love it."

Toni closed her eyes. And smiled.

FREEDOM

They say in vino veritas. Well, it's sure true that a bottle of wine and a few Mai Tais will kinda make you feel like, you know, just go for it! Or was it the seven-year itch? My wife Jennie and I *had* been married about seven years. All I know is that Freedée walked up to me in the downtown Papeete gallery, put her hand on my shoulder, stretched up to my ear, and whispered, "My name is Freedée. That means freedom." Then she licked my ear—only a little flick. I just stood there. In shock, I guess. She grabbed my arm and started to show me around the paintings.

Well. Freedée. There she was. Five foot three inches of bronze-skinned, black-haired, dark-eyed Tahitian ... energy. She looked just like the woman on a South Seas calendar that, as a teenager, I'd pinned on my bedroom wall back in Cleveland. When Jennie and I married and got our own place, she let me keep the picture tacked up in the garage next to my workbench.

Freedée stopped. "This one's of me," she said, pointing to a beautiful nude. "The artist is a friend of mine. Are you an artist? Maybe you'd like to paint me? Think you're up to it?"

What did she mean by that? Was that a kind of, you know, racy joke? I sort of hedged my bets in answering. "I think so, I guess, if I understand you, that is."

"So you do talk," she purred.

"Yes, I do," I said proudly. I was feeling pretty good.

I should tell you my name. It's Gerry Smythe, a common name, except for the spelling. I think the "y" and the "e" give it a touch of class. But I'm really just an ordinary guy, I guess. I've been a loan officer in a bank for eight years. Not a very exciting job, but it's stable. In these crazy times, it's good to have an anchor you can trust. You know, meat and potatoes on the table, and next month's rent pretty much guaranteed.

I'd dreamed of Tahiti ever since I got the calendar with the picture of that bare-breasted woman lying on the sand at the edge of an amazing blue lagoon. Not too many topless Tahitians in Cleveland. Except for maybe at Cheetahs, but I certainly don't go there. So, finally, there I was. Jennie and I'd saved enough to take a seven-day, six-night vacation package to Tahiti. The first night, we'd seen a Tahitian dance show at the hotel. Man! Can those women move their hips! And the men, all that knee wobbling and thrusting! The whole thing's, well, you know, kinda suggestive. Probably wouldn't go over too well with our church group, but Jennie didn't seem to mind. She's such a good sport.

Speaking of the hotel, we loved the place. We even took pictures of the all-you-can-eat dinner buffet. Anyway, our second night in Papeete, we decided to check out the local art scene. And now this thing with Freedée was happening. I'm sure it's every man's fantasy. So what was wrong with this picture? You've probably guessed by now. Jennie. She had just returned from the bathroom, and was now standing about 20 feet from us, staring.

I'm sure it was the alcohol's fault. We'd shared a bottle of French wine at a very late lunch around the hotel pool. The sun warmed our skin right through the canvas umbrella. After lunch, even with a coffee, I felt a little high. Back in our room, I'd hoped Jennie and I would maybe, you know … but she wanted to take a nap. So I went back down to the lobby, and read a book for a couple hours.

Just before sunset, we took a shower, then set out for our walk. A bar on the waterfront had a late happy hour, so each of us had a Mai Tai. It was a beautiful scene. Just the two of us, sitting there watching the surf break way out on the reef. We left the bar, and thanks to the trusty tourist map from the hotel, we found the gallery we were looking for.

I love the way Jennie looked that evening. She had on a pair of tight white pants and a dark blue camisole kinda thing with a light purple Tahitian shawl over her shoulders. And she was wearing the dangly silver earnings that give her the gypsy look I like.

But, back to Freedée. Obviously, I should have pried loose from her then and there, as soon as I saw Jennie. I should have told Freedée I was married—I was wearing a ring—and pointed out Jennie as my wife. But, no. I didn't. Anyway, I guess I was somewhat miffed at Jennie. I felt she was sort of taking me for granted. I mean, we're in Tahiti, and she wants to take a *nap*? Okay, so maybe she wants a more exciting life than a banker can provide. But I'm tall, still slim, reddish hair. I've always thought of myself as a California surfer kinda guy. So what the hell. Sometimes, you know, you gotta take the bull by the horns. Why not play out this scene with Freedée a little? Show Jennie that I'm still attractive to *other* women. At least *some* other women. Well, *one* other woman. Apparently.

As Freedée began to explain another painting to me, she slipped her arm around my waist. At that, Jennie crossed the room and calmly planted herself right in front of the painting. She smiled at us, a big grin, but didn't say a word. Just looked at us, smiling. Freedée looked her up and down. Of course, this was another moment for me to introduce Jennie, to explain the situation. Instead, I just stood there.

Freedée glared at Jennie. "Who are you?" she said, crisply enunciating each word.

Jennie looked at me. "Tell the nice lady, Gerald."

"Ah, yes. Of course. Freedée, I've been meaning to mention this to you. This is my wife, Jennie."

"You brought your *wife* to Tahiti?"

Jennie took a couple steps toward Freedée and crossed her arms. "He didn't *bring* me. We came here together. For a vacation," Jennie said, a cat playing with a mouse before biting its head off.

But Freedée was no mouse. You couldn't easily intimidate her. She tightened her arm around my waist. "So, American woman, you like the islands? The hot sun? The delicious, cool water? Sexy, no?" Jennie didn't answer.

"Oh, yes, she loves it," I said, casually trying to make Freedée's arm go away from my waist. But she held on.

"My name is Freedée," she said to Jennie. "That means freedom."

"Oh really? My name's Jennie. That means marriage."

Freedée laughed out loud. "That's okay. You in Tahiti." She pointed to a handsome Tahitian man who was smiling at us from across the room. "You like him? He's a gift!"

Jennie just stood there, staring at Freedée.

Then Freedée gave this truly carnivorous smile. "You Americans, you make everything so complicated. You always have to say *I love you*. What's that? Three words. Here, we just say *you, me—we go*."

"That's four words," said Jennie.

But Freedée was amazing. She laughed again. "Come with me," she said, and grabbed Jennie's arm. "I show you both a great bar. The owner's a friend of mine."

We left the gallery and walked along the harbor past the yachts and the occasional rusty, inter-island cargo ship, then turned a sharp right off Boulevard Pomare and headed inland. Freedée had let go of my waist—I guess we were on neutral territory—but she constantly grabbed my arm to focus me on every point of interest we walked past. And even some points without much interest. About three blocks in, we saw the Turtle Bar. It was behind a dirt parking lot that was occupied by a few old cars and a couple of taxi stands.

"Henri is a good friend," said Freedée as we entered. The bar was in full swing. It seemed a bit early, but I guess we were on island time. She led us to a table in the back corner and yelled out to the owner. "Henri, three Mai Tais! Make them special for me."

I looked around. It was a pretty cool place. Kinda like I'd always imagined after seeing that movie, *South Pacific*. The long, dark bar was filled with Tahitians drinking from brown beer bottles. Behind the bar were cartoon drawings of beautiful island women, each backlit—I notice these things—casting a sexy glow from the backbar out to the rattan bar stools. The walls were covered with nets decorated with big glass turtles and seashells lit from within, which gave the room a kind of underwater feeling. Other lights that looked like translucent fish were suspended on chains from the ceiling, fish head down. Each fish cast a tiny spot of light on a table. A small outrigger canoe was also hanging from the ceiling. Local pop music was blaring from the sound system.

And the customers! Wow, what a crowd. All Tahitian! The women were gorgeous—most of them dressed in bikini tops and tight short shorts or those sarong-type things slit up to the hip. Man, were they sexy! I just don't have enough words to describe them. I must admit that the men were also pretty attractive. All smiles and gleaming white teeth. Many of them were bare-chested, wearing only loose-fitting cotton pants. Their bodies were lean and tan with muscles like Olympic swimmers. A few of them even wore those sarong things wrapped kinda like shorts. I don't think that would look good on me though. Maybe on Jennie. What a crew! Nothing like this place in Ohio.

"*Bon soir, mes amis*," said Henri as he deposited three vats of some rum concoction on our table. He winked at Freedée, then walked back to the bar. So far, Jennie hadn't said a word. But after a few sips of her Mai Tai, she seemed to thaw out a little.

The music switched to Tahitian drums. The rapid beat was hypnotic. It reminded me of the music in the show at the hotel. Have you ever watched the women doing a Tahitian hula? How can they move their hips so fast? And the men! But I've already told you about the dancing.

The next song was a guitar ballad that made you see the soft moonlight on the lagoon, feel the sea breeze sighing through the palm trees, and smell the sweet perfume of frangipani. It made me feel kinda poetic. Freedée leaned real close to me, and I realized the perfume was really hers.

She caught the eye of a Tahitian Greek-god type in the crowd, and motioned him over. "This is Tiko," she said to Jennie. "He's beautiful, no?"

But Jennie wasn't falling for any of Freedée's charm.

"Hey, American woman, you like him?" cooed Freedée. "He's yours. I give him to you, a present." Freedée laughed as she again encircled my waist with her arm.

Now, I must say that Jennie looked pretty good. Tiko gave a nervous smile, but he did give Jennie an appreciative and pretty long once-over. He said something in Tahitian to Freedée, which made her laugh.

"Come on, American woman! You want to dance? I get Tiko to dance with you," urged Freedée.

"Not now, thank you, Freedée," Jennie answered icily. "But I'm sure he's very nice."

I guess Jennie didn't want to embarrass Tiko. He just smiled, nodded to all of us, turned and strolled back to the bar.

"Henri, mon ami, encore trois Mai Tais, s'il te plaît," Freedée yelled.

I'd studied a bit of French in high school, so I knew she was ordering more drinks. A beautiful barmaid danced her way through the crowd to deliver them to us. As she leaned over to put the drinks on the table, her breasts were right in front of my face. Oh, my. Yes, ma'am. But I didn't lose my cool. I didn't embarrass anyone.

"*Merci, merci,*" I said, keeping my eyes pretty much on my drink.

The barmaid flashed me a smile and giggled as she walked away, her hips swaying like—like—like hips. Lovely, luscious, Tahitian hips.

Freedée motioned to another Olympian-type local guy, who sauntered over to us, grinning all the way.

"Hey, American woman, this is Pierre, my cousin. He's beautiful, no? I give him to you. He's a gift."

As Jennie glanced up at Pierre's rippling muscles, Freedée's hand moved under the table to the front of my tropical-type shorts. They're my favorite travel shorts, khaki with, you know, big pockets on the sides. Well, I guess I was beginning to feel the effects of the rum because I let her keep her hand there. I suppose I even sort of encouraged her by casually moving around a little, all the while seeming to be completely involved in the meeting with Pierre.

"Freedée," Jennie said, "I'm just not in the mood to dance right now. But you're right, he's quite beautiful."

My turn to smile. I guess Jennie was starting to feel the rum, too.

Suddenly Freedée whipped her hand away from my shorts and grabbed my arm. "Let's dance, handsome!"

Good grief. I wasn't ready to get up from the table with the obvious bulge in my light khaki shorts. To gain time, I pretended to consider the idea while thinking frantically of cold showers, broccoli or mowing the lawn. I also wanted to see what Jennie was going to say. She just pursed her lips and sighed.

Freedée stood up and grabbed Jennie and me by the hand. She pushed Jennie over to Pierre and the four of us moved onto the tightly packed dance floor. The rum, the music, the crowd of bodies pressing together and swaying, the soft glow of the lights in the warm tropical air. It all began to carry me away. Even Jennie seemed to be having a good time. When the music stopped, she was standing next to Freedée and me. Freedée wrapped her arms around us both, bringing our faces close together. She looked appreciatively at Jennie and said, "You are very beautiful, American woman. Not physically, but inside."

Jennie pulled away. "That's it! I'm tired," she spat. "I'm going back to the hotel. And you, dear husband, do whatever you damn please." With that, she marched out from under the suspended outrigger, through the crowd, past the nets and turtles and shells, and out the door into the parking lot.

"Hey, Jennie, wait. I'll go, too," I called after her. But my legs seemed a bit numb. I guess I wasn't quick enough. Okay, be that way, I thought. Just when we were all having fun.

Freedée quickly sat me back down at the table. "It's late, not safe. She's a nice lady. I take care of her. You stay here."

Freedée dashed out the door. It seemed only a moment and she was back at my side. I must have nodded off while she was gone. Another ballad was playing. The couples were dancing close, very close. Freedée guided me again into the midst of the rhythmically moving bodies that swayed like a kelp forest in a gentle surf. She glued herself to me. All too soon, the music stopped.

"You want to see my place?" she whispered.

Now I began to panic. I'd never intended to let things get this far, had I? But let's face it. Freedée was dynamite. Without waiting for an answer, she took my hand and led me out of the Turtle Bar.

Freedée's beach shack was only a few blocks away. And only a few yards or so off the shore of the lagoon. You could hear the breeze rustling the palms and the wavelets bubbling over the sand. Inside, Freedée lit a few candles, and then put on a disc of very soft island songs. It was a one-room cottage. A counter separated the tiny kitchen from the living room/bedroom. A large bed with fluffy white pillows was set against the wall.

"Make yourself at home. I be right back," and she disappeared into the bathroom.

I know, I know, I know. Leave, now, I said to myself. But I was curious. Was this really happening to me? How would I feel if I left? How would I feel if I stayed? What would Jennie say if I got back to the hotel so late? But Freedée was my dream. Was I going to chicken out? Was I afraid to see it through? Which was more frightening—to stay or to leave? My last ditch attempt to depart was snuffed out when Freedée re-entered the room.

Her sarong thing sat loosely on her hips. She moved through the dancing shadows with tiny steps, arms held out to me, lips smiling, eyes glistening, bare breasts gently swaying, swaying ... swaying. There she was, my living calendar woman in the all too lovely flesh.

Well, Jesus, Mary, and Joseph! Might as well be hung for a sheep as a lamb. Jennie's mad as hell anyway. No matter what I do now, she's gonna kill me. This means I'm free. I have to face the consequences either way, don't I?

Freedée continued to move toward me, arms outstretched. In a moment, we were dancing in a close embrace. A moment later, we were next to her bed. Okay, gentlemen. So, what would you have done?

You don't need an alarm clock in Tahiti. There are roosters everywhere that proudly crow at the first hint of sunrise. I woke up to the strident bragging of a couple of noisy fowl outside the window. My dreams during a few hours' sleep had been a kaleidoscope of turtles innocently swimming in the tropical surf, and luminous fish hanging from the sky. All in a matrix of swaying hips, luscious breasts, and white teeth. But now, across the bottom of my internal TV screen, there was a message warning me that I couldn't avoid getting up forever. Gone were the ballads, the waves, the guitars, the whole nighttime mood. The only drums were a constant throbbing inside my head. I was afraid to open my eyes. When I finally did, there was Freedée, lying peacefully beside me.

She opened her eyes, and grinned. "You want some coffee before you go?" she asked in a matter-of-fact way.

"Oh, no thanks, that's very kind of you," I said as I bounced up and threw on my clothes. "I've got to get going."

I walked through the empty streets for a mile or so, then cut through the park and back to the hotel on the shore. I barely noticed the yachts, the cargo boats and the early morning fishermen casting their circular nets from the water's edge. Once in the lobby, I walked slowly to the elevator, but then I lost my nerve. I turned around and sat down behind the unoccupied desk of the agent who sold sunset sailing tours.

Head in hands, elbows on the glass, I stared out the open-air front entrance at the green fields and hills beyond the curved asphalt driveway. I had to regroup. The idea of running right up to the room and confronting Jennie terrified me. So there I sat, dumping buckets of guilt—just a metaphor—over my head. What was I going to tell her? Lie? Say I passed out on Freedée's floor the instant we got back to her place? Or tell the truth and blame it on the alcohol? I could always grovel and swear that it was only a drunken aberration that would never happen again. Oh, God! What was I thinking? How could I have done this to Jennie? My chest began to heave with repressed sobs. What would I see in her eyes? Hurt? Sadness? Anguish? A wound that would take forever to heal? A deep ache that my idiocy had created? Or maybe anger, spite, even hatred. No doubt, my callous selfishness would soon be the talk of Jennie's book club.

Outside, the breakfast waiter and a couple of long-haired waitresses jumped down from *le truck,* a sort of combination open-air bus and flatbed truck that roams the island with no apparent schedule. It picks up passengers whenever someone waves it down. I remembered that Jennie and I rode *le truck* the day we arrived. It took us all over the town, along the lagoon road, and even a bit into the jungle interior of the island. We stayed aboard for a round trip. Back in downtown Papeete, we walked hand-in-hand through the colorful market, a mass of stalls clustered beneath a corrugated iron roof. We stared at the cages of clucking chickens, the piles of strange fish—bright red, green, pearl, mouths wide open, eyes staring. Next to the fish were tables of freshly butchered goats. We saw stands heaped with coconuts, tropical fruit, vegetables, eggs, butter, woven baskets and straw hats. And huge coolers filled with bottles of Hinano, the local beer. We were so happy. So excited to be having this adventure in a tropical paradise. Together.

So, idiot! Look at you now, I said to myself. The home breaker. The heartless male butterfly that cares only about himself. You have no excuses. Jennie, the poor darling, coming back to the hotel alone at night, feeling deserted by her brute of a husband. Abandoned in paradise.

Then I really got scared. What's Jennie going to do now. Divorce me? I'd never felt so desolate, so dumb. I had to do something.

The town was now awake. Guests were filtering downstairs and heading to the breakfast buffet. I stood up. Better to face her in the room, not in the lobby.

A cab pulled up to the front entrance. The driver, another Greek god, hopped out of the car and opened the door for his passenger. A lady got out, gave him a peck on the cheek, and waved as the cab pulled away. She turned and walked into the lobby. Oh no! It was Jennie! She woke up early. I wasn't there. She got worried and went out looking for me. How could I ever make this right?

Then she saw me. My heart fell through the floor. Was she going to make a scene right here in the lobby? No. She smiled brightly and walked toward me. God, she looked so sexy in those white pants. She must not have slept. She hadn't even changed her clothes. She stopped in front of me. I bravely looked her in the eye.

"How are you today?" she said.

"I'm okay. How are you? ... And who's that guy who drove you up here?"

"You mean André? He's a gift—from Freedée."

MEN AND DOGS

Erik woke up to the sudden pain of five daggers stabbing into his left shoulder. Sheila had plunged her razor-sharp fingernails into his naked, defenseless body. He twisted away from her and leaped from the bed. All the room lights were on. Beads of blood welled up and began to slowly trickle down his arm. "What the hell …" he gasped.

Sheila glared at him. "Two things I hate most," she hissed. "Men and dogs!"

Sheila was a recent acquaintance. Shortly after Erik arrived in Torremolinos, he met her in the bar Corazón where she worked. She was hard to miss. Her long dark hair and tight black T-shirt had immediately attracted his attention. Even in the dim light, if one looked closely—and most men did—the words "DON'T YOU WISH" were visible, emblazoned in pink letters across her chest. Large gold hoop earrings framed her face, and her deep red lipstick accentuated every movement of her full lips. Her dark eyes were heavily outlined in black. A single gold bracelet hung loosely on her left wrist. Her fingernails were long and carefully painted to match her lipstick. She worked efficiently, but her walk was a feline prowl, seemingly relaxed, but alert.

As Sheila neared his end of the bar, Erik ordered: "*Un ron y coke, por favor.*" She glanced at him and nodded. The moody strains of "A Whiter Shade of Pale" glided through the room, and caressed the clinging couples that danced slowly in the shadowy space between the bar and the small round tables set against the opposite wall. The aroma of sex mixed with perfume and cigarette smoke blended with the hot, salty Mediterranean night air.

Erik had been in Spain for a month. His lean six-foot frame, blue eyes, and sandy hair suggested northern European heritage. His ready smile and perpetually relaxed posture identified him as an American. Sheila brought him his drink, then stood across the bar from him and began to dry some glasses. Outgoing and friendly, Erik usually had no trouble chatting with new people. But Sheila short-circuited this ability. Erik watched her polish each glass. Yes, Sheila's proximity unnerved him. Pheromone overload? Worry that his Spanish was too poor? Or, like Prufrock, was he just afraid? A jumble of literary references jostled in Erik's brain as he tried to subdue the rush of attraction he felt. He couldn't take his eyes off her.

Sheila set some glasses on the backbar, turned, and looked directly at him. "Hi," she said.

"Hi. *Como se llama usted?*"

"Try English."

Erik laughed. "Okay, one obstacle gone. What's your name?"

"Sheila."

"Mine's Erik."

"Good for you." She picked up another glass.

"Well, I'll try another original opening. Where are you from?"

"I'm Greek, but I grew up in London."

"London! A great city. I've got some friends there." Erik radiated enthusiasm.

"And I've got work to do," she said, and walked away.

Erik watched her serve other customers. He couldn't

help but notice how nicely her faded jeans fit her. As he sipped his rum and coke, Erik often checked to see if she lingered with any particular male. He was gratified to note that she seemed all business.

Eventually she came back to Erik. "Want another drink?"

"Yeah, sounds great."

Sheila poured him a large amount of rum followed by a splash of coke. "On the house," she said with a smile.

"Thanks." Erik's system began to adjust to the additional adrenaline Sheila's presence inspired. "Let me repay you," he suggested.

Her smile reappeared. "Oh? You have something I need?" She started to polish another glass.

"No. I mean, how about lunch ... a picnic? Tomorrow afternoon."

"You think so?"

"Yes. On the beach. We can get to know each other."

Sheila stared at him for a moment. "Get to know each other. Sure."

"Let's meet in the square outside the bar at two."

Abruptly, she took a step back. To Erik's surprise, she appeared to be blushing. "Thank you. See you tomorrow," she whispered, and turned away.

The following afternoon at two o'clock, Erik stood in front of the Corazón, joyfully observing the crowded plaza. He loved Torremolinos. The hot, dusty streets had a vibrant rhythm that filled him with energy. Every morning, he awoke to the excitement of the unknown. What would happen today? Where would he go? Who would he meet? Everything was possible. He was sure that Passion and Beauty awaited him around every corner. All he had to do was look.

Indeed, Erik loved all of southern Spain. It's brilliant blue sky, fierce sun, gentle Mediterranean surf, long sandy beaches, palm trees rustling in the hot wind, rolling brown grassy hills dotted with olive trees, and the ubiquitous billboard silhouettes of the iconic Osborne Sherry black bull. Erik delighted in the flower-filled courtyards, the burbling fountains, and the sultry evenings when the streets of every town filled with people and the myriad cafes were packed with noisy crowds. And the music. Andalusia, the cradle of *flamenco puro*.

But in spite of his current happiness, Erik often brooded about his brief, ill-advised marriage. His recent divorce was amicable, but still painful. They'd both been way too young. He knew it. But he told himself—

with more than a dollop of melodrama—that he'd never again let a woman get that close.

He glanced across the square at the two tall palms standing in front of the hotel Casa de la Luna, a three-story stucco building. Once a week, he would treat himself to a *tortilla española* and a half bottle of dry rosé in the Luna's air-conditioned cafe. He'd been very annoyed to learn that the hotel would soon be torn down to make room for a high-rise apartment building. Erik continued to scan the plaza. No sign of her yet. Don't be impatient, he told himself.

Around two-thirty, Sheila emerged from a narrow side street and wandered through the crowd toward him. Erik suppressed the urge to run out and meet her. Eventually, she neared the Corazón. Only then did Sheila appear to notice him. Her face remained without expression. "So, you're here."

"You thought I wouldn't be?"

"I don't know. I don't take anything for granted."

"Me neither." Erik held up his picnic sack. "Shall we go?"

"Sure."

Erik and Sheila strolled through the old town along cobbled streets flanked by whitewashed apartment buildings, and down the steep steps to the beach. They passed through a line of palm trees and crossed to the water's edge. Erik spread two beach mats on the hot sand. Sheila peeled off her shorts and T-shirt to reveal a skimpy red bikini.

Erik had spent much of the morning combing the markets for his picnic provisions. He proudly set out large cuts of *jamón Serrano*, a small jar of olives, a wedge of manchego, a crusty loaf of bread, and two heavy wine glasses he'd brought from his kitchen. With a flourish, he presented a bottle of *Penedès blanco*. Sheila observed his preparation with a faint smile.

They sat side by side, lounging in the hot sun, sipping wine, watching the gentle surf.

"What are you doing in Torremolinos?" Sheila asked.

"I'm living here, at least for now."

"Do you work?"

"Of course. I teach English."

She nodded. "How long will you stay?"

"I'm not sure. Half a year, maybe more. And you?"

"I don't know. I like it here."

Erik raised his glass. "Here's to Torremolinos."

"To Torremolinos," she said, returning his toast.

"So tell me about your family in London."

"You don't want to know," Sheila muttered. She seemed more than a little annoyed at Erik's suggestion.

This puzzled him, but he persisted. "Sure I do. Tell me."

Sheila grimaced. "My dad's a plumber."

"And your mom?"

"Dead." Sheila popped an olive into her mouth.

"I'm sorry."

"Don't be," she said, with a dismissive shrug.

"Well, any brothers or sisters?"

"Yeah. A younger brother and an older sister."

"I've got a kid brother, too. What's yours like?"

"He used to be left-handed."

"Used to be? What happened?"

"Papa cured him."

"*Cured* him?"

"Papa's old fashioned. He thinks left-handers are stupid. Alex was four years old; Papa bashed his hand against a brick wall 'til Alex couldn't use it. Now he's right-handed."

"Jesus," Erik muttered.

Sheila stared at the sea. Erik poured more wine. They sipped the cool *vino blanco*.

After a few moments, Sheila carefully set her glass on the sand. Without a word, she rested her head on Erik's shoulder and began to lightly run her fingertips along his forearm. Slowly, from the wrist to the elbow, back again to the wrist. "I'm sorry. I didn't mean to be such a downer," she said quietly. Sheila's touch sent a jolt of electricity throughout Erik's body. Her abrupt change of mood surprised him. Mercurial woman, he thought. But I certainly like her the way she is now. He closed his eyes. She continued to move her fingertips back and forth along his arm.

Suddenly Sheila laughed and picked up her glass. "Here we are in southern Spain in the hot sun. This is good."

"You're right," he said. They touched glasses and knocked back the rest of the wine.

Still laughing, Sheila stood up, removed her bikini top and plunged into the water. Erik promptly followed her into the surf. She grabbed his hand and pulled him into an oncoming wave. They rolled together in the water like two playful seal pups. Sheila's aquatic antics revealed that she was remarkably strong. After a few moments, they swam slowly away from the shore into the cooler deep water. As they lazily floated together, Erik looped his arm around her waist and drew her to him. She didn't resist his kiss, but Erik felt the tension in her body.

"You don't want me to kiss you?"

"Sure I do, but ... I'm sorry."

He slowly slid his arm away from her waist, and hid his disappointment behind a gentle smile. They floated together for a while longer, and then swam back to the shore.

They lay on the mats next to one another and dried off in the sun. The shadows of the palm trees slowly lengthened. After a while, Erik sat up. "Shall we get a coffee?" he suggested. They put on their T-shirts and shorts. Sheila threw her dry bikini top into the picnic sack. After strapping on their sandals, they strolled across the sand to a nearby beach bar. They sat on clammy, canvas folding chairs, the cloth rotten with salt, sweat, and suntan oil. They watched the waves.

"Do you like the sea?" Erik asked.

"Never thought much about it."

"I love it. I love to be out on a ship. And I love to watch the water from shore, especially at night. '… the lone line of spray / Where the sea meets the moon-blanch'd sand.' Dover Beach." Erik liked to quote snippets of poetry. But to his credit, he wasn't entirely oblivious to Sheila's lack of response. Okay, so much for Matthew Arnold. "So, Sheila, you've been here awhile?"

"About six months."

"Got a boyfriend?"

"Just a sailor now and then." She didn't seem pleased with the topic.

"A sailor now and then," laughed Erik. "Reminds me of a friend of mine when I was an undergrad. Old Arnie. He was in Navy ROTC. After his first summer at sea, he laughed at the rest of us and called us 'boys.' That was before I got married."

"Oh? You're married?"

"Divorced. We were too young. Getting married was a stupid thing to do. After a year, she found a boyfriend. Big deal. I was no saint. I wanted out, too. But I still feel responsible for her."

"You'll get over it." Clearly, Sheila wasn't interested.

"Anyway, as I was saying, old Arnie said we *boys* complicate things. That all you really have to do is find a bar, pick up a woman, then it's back to her place or a hotel and that's all there is to it."

Sheila's face twisted as if she'd just bitten into a lemon. "Of course, that's all men are interested in. Sex."

This archaic cliché and the attitude it revealed surprised Erik, especially coming from Sheila. "Well. Guess I've heard that before."

"It's true."

"Not always."

"Then why are you talking to me?"

"I mean the *all* part."

"What's that supposed to mean?"

Erik began to feel that talking to Sheila was like trying to converse with a cactus. He winced at the simile, but persisted in his explanation. "Look, it's not always *all* that men want. I used to argue with Arnie. I've never been able to pick up someone and hop into bed before I even know her name. And I certainly didn't mean to suggest anything negative to you."

"So you think you're different?"

"No, maybe not," he said slowly. "I can't say I'm different. I guess I just like to get to know someone. And I do think erotic love is a good thing." Erik preferred words like "eros," "desire," or "passion," to the simple monosyllable "sex." He often defended this preference. But he didn't want to argue with Sheila. "I just mean it's supposed to be mutual pleasure, not mortal combat."

"How poetic." The lemon look remained.

"You don't think so?"

"Think what?"

"That it's supposed to make you happy, not angry."

"If you say so." The lemon look dissolved into a sullen frown. "Men can do anything they damn please. But I stay out late one night, and suddenly I'm a whore."

"I don't think that way."

"Well you should have a talk with my Papa."

Erik was baffled. Of course he wanted Sheila. Since

last night and all day long—in living color—he'd imagined them together. And he wanted her to feel the same about him. But what could he do? Any move now and she would scorn him. Just another male lusting after her crotch. And Erik couldn't bring himself to regard sex as a martial art. "Look, I didn't mean to upset you."

"Don't talk about it. Think what you want. *Do* what you want. Just don't talk about it."

Do what I want, he thought? Is that an invitation? But to what? To justify her contempt? Or to just screw her and skip the chatter, as Arnie would say? Erik was often mired in such futile, internal dialectic. And he was clearly out of sync with Sheila. The relationship was not going the way he'd hoped it would. "Okay," he said. "But just let me explain a bit."

As he began to launch into his theories about the romance of life, a large black dog bounded across the sand and into the surf. A few leaps and splashes, and the dog bounced out of the water. It shook itself, and then romped toward their table. Sheila gasped and grabbed Erik's hand.

"What's the matter?"

"A dog," she said in a strangled voice. Sheila's eyes never left the animal as it loped by them and wandered off down the beach.

"You don't like dogs?"

"I got bit once. I threw out some garbage in the neighbors' bin. Their damn German shepherd bit me." Sheila pointed toward her calf. Erik hadn't noticed the scars.

"I'm sorry," he said.

"Why? It's not your fault."

They watched the dog ramble along the water's edge until it disappeared behind some faraway rocks. Sheila began to relax. They sipped their coffee.

"What brought you to Torremolinos?" Erik asked.

"It was Papa."

Erik winced at the acid in her voice. There's Papa again. "Papa? Tell me about it."

"Why do you care?"

"I'm interested, that's all."

"Later."

"You don't believe me?"

"Look, I have to get ready for work soon."

"Okay. That's fine." Don't argue with her, Erik told himself.

It was almost sunset. They finished their coffee, headed back up the steps and walked along the streets toward Sheila's apartment. Erik put his arm around her shoulder. She didn't seem to mind. They strolled through a square surrounded by cafes and restaurants with outdoor tables. The tapas bars were just beginning to fill with customers.

"Do you ever get a night off?"

Sheila considered her response. "Yeah. Now and then." She gave a laugh. "The boss likes me."

The boss likes her? What does that mean? Oh come now, Erik, he cautioned. Don't get jealous. You have no reason, and no right, to react that way. They reached her apartment, a tiny one-bedroom above a pizza restaurant on a street filled with motor scooter traffic.

"A bit noisy here, isn't it?"

"Yeah, but it's cheap. And it quiets down around four in the morning."

"Do you have a roommate?"

"Uh-huh. She works in a Japanese restaurant. She's usually asleep when I get back."

Erik gave Sheila a gentle hug. "Maybe see you tonight?" he asked quietly.

"Sure. *Un ron y coke*?" She smiled and kissed him on the cheek.

Late that night, Erik was back at the Corazón. To the slow pulse of "Nights in White Satin," the swaying couples urged their bodies ever closer, rhythmically drifting in and out of pools of light in the densely packed room. Sheila nodded to him and brought him a rum and coke. Her left hand was wrapped in a dirty bar rag dotted with dark red patches.

"What happened to you?" Erik asked as he picked up his drink.

"Nothing."

"Nothing? Then what's that on your hand?"

"Nothing important. It'll be fine." She flashed an automatic smile.

Erik set his drink on the bar. "What will be fine?" he asked. Sheila let Erik take her wrist, turn her hand over and carefully remove the bloody cloth. He shuddered at the ugly, deep wound in the center of her palm. She'd accidentally impaled her hand on the jagged neck of a broken beer bottle. "You better see a doctor quick. That could become very nasty."

She pulled her hand away. "It'll be fine. It doesn't matter. Besides, doctors cost money."

"I know where there's a decent clinic that's cheap. It's even free if you can't pay." Sheila grabbed two empty glasses with her good hand and walked off toward the sink. "I'll come by your apartment in the morning and take you there," Erik called across the bar.

"Don't bother. It's not worth it," she shot back

over her shoulder. She began to serve drinks to other customers.

Erik finished his rum and coke. "See you tomorrow," he said, and moved toward the door. Sheila just waved, not looking at him. Erik went home. He didn't sleep well that night.

At nine the following morning, Sheila's roommate, a young Japanese woman, opened the door for Erik. "I'm here to pick up Sheila," he said. The woman nodded and glanced toward the couch. "She says she won't get up."

Sheila, wrapped tightly in a blanket up to her chin, lay there staring at the two of them. When Erik finally got her to bring her hand out from beneath the blanket, it was wrapped in the same dirty bar rag, now caked all over with dried blood. "Just let me have a look," he said. Slowly, he pried the rag away from her hand. An angry red ring was spreading outward from the wound. "Okay, let's go. The clinic it is. No arguments." He tugged Sheila off the couch. She still had her work clothes on.

"What are you doing?" Sheila asked.

"Taking you to get that hand treated."

"Why do you care? It's my hand."

"You want me to just leave you alone?"

Sheila frowned. "No. I guess not."

Erik nudged her along for the half-mile walk to the clinic. As they approached the building, she stopped. "What's the matter, Sheila? You afraid of clinics?"

"Not afraid. I don't like them. And I don't like doctors."

"Why not?"

"I told you."

"You told me what?"

"About my sister and the paper bag!"

Erik stopped and looked at her. "I don't know what you're talking about."

"It wasn't garbage when the dog bit me. It was my sister's."

"Your sister's what?"

"It was from my sister's baby."

"What?"

"Her baby!" And she poured out the story.

At 17, her sister had become pregnant. She'd managed to hide this fact from Papa. Early in the pregnancy, she was somehow able to induce a miscarriage in the bedroom she shared with Sheila. Sheila's sister wiped up the blood with a towel and put the fetus in a paper bag. She gave it to Sheila with instructions to flush the fetus down the toilet. Sheila, fearing for her life, crept past

Papa who was having a beer while watching TV. She went into the bathroom and followed her sister's orders. Later that day, while Papa was working, the two girls crumpled the blood-soaked towel into the same paper bag and threw it in a neighbor's trash bin. As they turned to leave, Sheila was bitten by the neighbor's vigilant German shepherd.

"So I went to the clinic to get my leg stitched up," Sheila continued. "The doctor made me take off my pants."

"Well, the doctor had to see the bite."

"Yeah, but he touched me."

"Well, what was he supposed to do? Somehow examine the wound *without* touching you?"

"Yeah, but he touched me a long way from where the dog bit me."

They walked up to the clinic in silence.

Inside, Sheila sat stiffly as the nurse cleaned and disinfected the wound, and then carefully bandaged Sheila's hand with sterile gauze and tape. "Don't get the bandage wet," she warned Sheila. The nurse gave her a shot in the arm, and told her to come back the next day. Sheila faintly sneered.

Erik took her back to her flat. "Get some rest," he said. "I'll see you tonight."

He arrived late in the evening. Sheila promptly brought him a glass of rum. She laughed as she splashed in a bit of coke. The entire bandage was now pink, soaked through with water.

"Nice going, Sheila. You got the bandage all wet. The nurse will *not* be happy tomorrow."

Sheila just looked at him and continued to work.

In the morning, Erik again took her to the clinic. The same nurse rebandaged the wound. "No more water on that bandage, you understand?" Erik said.

Sheila nodded. "Alright."

Erik walked her back to her flat. "How do you cook? I mean with only one hand."

"I don't."

"You want me to fix you lunch tomorrow?"

"Another picnic on the beach?"

"No. At my place. I'll give you the address. It's not far from here."

Sheila shrugged. "Sure."

"Are you still going to work tonight?" he asked.

"I have to."

"You promise to be careful?"

"Yes. I promise."

That night at the bar, Erik noticed that Sheila's wounded hand remained dry. "Please keep it that way."

"Yes, sir. See you tomorrow. Your place for lunch."

Erik's studio apartment was in an ancient, two-story building with tiny balconies, a shady courtyard, and very few cockroaches, as long as he carefully cleaned his kitchen every night and kept all food in the vintage refrigerator. He'd been lucky to find an affordable place near the beach. At night, he could hear the surf through his open bedroom window.

After his classes, Erik spent a pleasant hour shopping for food and wine, and thinking about Sheila. He wasn't blind to her flashes of sweetness, and he liked her rebellious spirit. He fancied himself a rebel, as indeed he was. A fortunate rebel. His main enemies were a rich, domineering uncle and the stifling pressure to "conform" in Erik's Babbitt-filled Midwestern hometown.

Sheila arrived with a large black tote bag on her shoulder and a portable record player in her hand. "Hi," she said cheerfully, and gave Erik a kiss on the cheek. She handed him the record player, set her bag on the floor, and pulled out several albums from beneath a makeup kit, her bikini, and a jumble of other garments. "I thought we might like some music. Maybe even dance."

"Sounds good." Erik liked the thought of holding her close. But after her guarded response to his kiss when they were swimming, he was determined to go very slowly. He wanted her to trust him, to see that he would never hurt her. There had to be at least *some* meaning to any eventual intimacy.

Erik put on a record and filled a small tray with plates of almonds and olives, half of a cold Spanish omelet, and a bottle of *Rioja*. They ate outside in the tiny courtyard.

"So what's your hometown like?" Sheila asked.

"Small, provincial, and boring. Nothing as exciting as London."

"And your family?"

"I get along well with my kid brother, and pretty well with my mom. I know my dad loves me, but there's a lot of conflict between us."

"Why is that?"

"He wants me to work for him and my uncle in the family business. I can't stand the idea. I guess I'll always disappoint my dad."

"Poor boy."

Her tone of voice surprised Erik. "Why are you being sarcastic? You asked me. I told you."

"Sorry."

Erik thought about Sheila's family for a moment. "The other day, you said your dad was the reason you're here."

"Did I?"

"Yeah."

"I guess I did. And he is the reason. In a way. Why do you want to know?"

"It's part of your history. I'm interested."

"Most men are more interested in my tits."

They are extraordinary, Erik thought. But, careful. Don't say it. Don't talk about it. "Look Sheila, you don't have to tell me." The music ended. Erik walked back into the apartment and changed the record.

As he settled himself back into his chair, Sheila gave him a puzzled look. "So you really want to know more about Papa?"

"I want to know more about *you*."

"Okay."

The story of Papa came out in fragments. Scrambled pieces of a dark puzzle. By the time Sheila finished, the record was long since over. "So now you know why I'm here."

"God, what a story. I'm sorry."

"Don't be," she said flatly. "It's all in the past. It doesn't matter."

"It *does* matter."

"Maybe for you, not for me."

Erik knew that wasn't true. He took a deep breath and exhaled slowly. "Well, anyway, I guess you put my own problems in perspective."

"I wouldn't know. What time is it?"

"It's after five."

"I have to get ready for work."

"Sure. I'll walk you over to your place. Just let me get your stuff."

"Leave it here. I'll get it some other time."

After Erik walked Sheila home, he wandered through the crowded streets. Eventually, he stopped to get a small dinner of tapas and cheap red wine. He couldn't get Sheila out of his mind—her fiery temperament, rapid mood shifts, mixed signals. She's a challenge, he thought. And her story about Papa. What a life. Reason enough to be defensive.

In her final year of high school, she'd said, she came home too late one night. Papa had gone through his usual number of pints at the local pub. When he got home, he discovered that Sheila was still out. Convinced his smart-mouthed daughter was up to no good, Papa decided to wait up for her. He consoled himself in his solitary vigil with a bottle of Retsina. When Sheila later sneaked into the entry hall, he stepped out of the darkened kitchen and greeted her by grabbing her hair. She fought back, but he forced her to the floor, and began to kick her in the stomach and face. "You just a goddamn whore!" he screamed. He grabbed her hair again, yanked her to her feet, and threw her out the front door onto the brick walk. "Bitch! Whore! You ever come back, I kill you!"

Papa was a man of his word. Sheila never returned. After two years of sleeping on the couches of various friends, at age 18, she'd wandered down to Torremolinos.

Erik spent the rest of the evening alone on the beach, listening to the waves as they softly crawled up the shore and then retreated. He looked at the stars and the lights from occasional passing ships, and sipped a cold bottle of *cava*. He knew that brutalizing women had been a male pastime throughout history. One could hardly attribute its invention to a Greek plumber living in modern London. Erik thought again of Matthew Arnold, and remembered there was a lot more to

"Dover Beach" than the calm imagery of moonbeams on the water. Fragments about waves bringing in "The eternal note of sadness" and about Sophocles hearing "the turbid ebb and flow / Of human misery." Surely Sheila would understand those lines.

And as he stared into the darkness, his late-night thoughts, as usual, drifted back to his ex-wife. Where was she now? How was she? And, dammit, why should he still feel responsible for her? Just because she's a woman? They both wanted the divorce. No blame on either side. It was nobody's fault. You'll get over it, Sheila said. But when?

Yes, Sheila. And Papa. She must see that I'm not like her dad. Suddenly, Erik remembered a trip to New Orleans he'd taken with a friend at age 15. They'd summoned the nerve to go into a strip club in the Latin Quarter. To their delight, they'd each been served a beer. Erik remembered that the young stripper on stage had a thick, jagged scar running across her belly. After the performance, she sat down at Erik's table. The boys bought her a beer, and they all talked for a few minutes. Erik's friend excused himself and headed for the bathroom. The woman finished her beer. As she got up to leave, she looked at Erik and frowned. "You're a nice kid," she said. "We'll see how long you stay that way."

The warm breeze rustled the leaves in the palm trees at the edge of the sand. Erik finished the bottle of *cava*.

Another two weeks passed. Sheila remained careful at work and didn't soak the bandage in dirty water. She seemed to be taking better care of herself, and she spent a lot of time at Erik's end of the bar. Sometimes she would meet him for coffee after he finished teaching for the day. They often had lunch at Erik's place. He still hadn't risked even kissing her again. And, to his alarm, Sheila continued to leave more of her things in his apartment.

"We should really take all your stuff home," he said one day. "It must be inconvenient for you to leave it here."

Sheila shrugged. "Why bother? I spend more time here than I do at my place. And I like it here."

What does that mean? Erik wondered. He wasn't ready to share life every day with someone. But he didn't voice his fears.

Sheila's wounded hand healed. The nurse removed the final bandage and smiled at the two of them. She didn't ask for payment. On the way back from the clinic, Erik suggested that Sheila have dinner with him the following evening. "I teach three classes in the morning, but I've got the rest of the day and the weekend free."

"I guess so," Sheila answered. "I'll tell my boss. He has extra girls working on the weekends anyway."

The following morning, after a quick instant coffee and a piece of stale bread with jam, Erik was on his way to his Friday lessons. As he passed the beach, he noticed that a large, gray naval vessel was anchored out in the bay.

His first language student was an anachronism in Torremolinos, a weathered 50-year-old Spaniard who still made his living as a fisherman in spite of the depleted sea and the wall of apartment buildings rising ever higher on shore. Why this man wanted to learn English was a mystery to Erik. Two attractive women from Brazil made up his second class. Their motives for staying in the class were clearly more than linguistic. Erik kept a professional distance in the face of persistent invitation. For Erik, neither of the women held the allure of Sheila. His third-hour student was a charming, elderly Spanish lady who always dressed in black and wore solid, sensible shoes. Her daughter now lived in New York City and had recently had a child. Grandma wanted to learn her grandson's language.

Classes over, Erik waved happily to the office secretary, and bounced down the stairs to the street. To his surprise, Sheila was waiting for him outside the school. "Hi, Sheila. I didn't expect to see you 'til tonight. C'mon, I need a decent coffee." He took her arm, and they headed for a tiny cafe a few blocks away.

"Yeah, about tonight," Sheila said.

"What about it?"

"Well, it's just that … maybe I can't come."

"Why not? Boss angry at you?"

"No. It's hard to explain."

Erik released her arm. "Well, give it a try. I'm a patient person."

"I just think … I don't know … and please, don't come to the bar this weekend."

He stopped walking. Even Erik, with his head in the clouds, began to see what was going on. "Tell me, could this change of plan have anything to do with the navy ship anchored off our fair shore?"

"So really, why do you care? You haven't made, you know, any moves."

"I got the strong impression you didn't want me to."

"What difference would that make?" Sheila muttered.

"*All* the difference." Sheila was silent. "So have a good time this weekend," Erik said.

"What does that mean?"

"It's pretty clear. It means have fun."

Sheila hesitated. "No, it doesn't. It means I won't see you again."

"Probably not." Erik started to leave.

Sheila grabbed his arm. "That's not fair."

"What's not fair?"

"You know what I mean!"

"All I know is that I was really looking forward to our evening together." He turned and headed for the cafe.

Sheila caught up with him. Slowly, they trudged along the shaded cobblestone street, past the whitewashed buildings with black wrought iron balconies overhung with masses of red and purple geraniums, an idyllic setting but for the constant, peevish whine of passing motor scooters.

They reached the cafe, a dark cavern with a few outside tables on a drab square surrounded by shabby apartment buildings whose balconies were hung with laundry. "I'll still buy you a cup of coffee," Erik said gently.

"Thank you." Sheila hesitated. "And will you still buy me dinner tonight?"

Erik picked her up at eight o'clock in the ancient Morris Minor convertible that he'd brought over from England. He drove Sheila through the hot Spanish night into Malaga. "We'll start with tapas and wine. This is my favorite bodega," said Erik as he ushered her into a dimly lit cave. Heavy oak barrels lined the wall behind the bar. Massive haunches of *jamón Serrano* hung from the ceiling. A mournful *Seguiriya* poured from two speakers mounted above the wine casks. Erik thought he recognized the music. "Listen. I think the *cantaor* is Aurelio de Cádiz, with Ramón Montoya on guitar. A real gypsy sound."

"I think it's strange music."

"It is. Strangely beautiful."

Sheila and Erik sat perched on high stools at a small round table, and sipped glasses of cool dry sherry.

"How's the hand?"

"It's fine now. Thanks to you."

"Come on. You don't need to thank me."

"I want to."

"Okay."

"Why'd you do it?" Sheila seemed genuinely puzzled.

"Do what?"

"Don't always be so difficult. You know what I mean."

"Why did I refuse to watch you become a candidate for amputation?"

"Yeah."

"I don't know. Maybe I like you. You might have guessed."

"Maybe I could guess that." She sipped her sherry and smiled.

"You know ... you know ... not all men are like your father."

Sheila's smile remained, but her eyes turned glacial. She put her wine glass on the table. Even in the dim light of the crowded bodega, Erik could see the reaction. "I didn't mean to say anything to make you feel bad, I just—"

Sheila reached out and placed two fingers on his lips. "Shhh, shhh, don't talk about it. Shhh. Learn silence. Yes, silence. Just drink the wine like that first day on the beach."

"You too," he said.

She picked up her glass. "Me too."

As they left the bodega, Sheila put her arm around

Erik's waist and pulled him close to her side.

They dined in a small, dark restaurant. The candles on the tables were stuck in old wine bottles, and the wax had dripped down the glass to form small, fantastically shaped sculptures. Erik ordered a paella for two and a bottle of red wine. After coffee, they strolled through the darkened city to a large, walled-in public park. It seemed closed for the night, but one of the heavy iron gates was unlocked. Erik took Sheila's hand and led her inside. The moon was full. The trees cast deep shadows across the gravel paths.

Beside a murmuring fountain, Erik stopped and turned to her. Sheila's perfume mingled with the sweet aroma of jasmine. He pulled her to him and kissed her. The strength of her response thrilled him. Erik was living a dream. Romance in an Andalusian garden at midnight with this beautiful woman. I've got past her tough shell, he thought. She trusts me. Sheila's dark hair flowed softly around her face and her eyes glistened in the moonlight. Their kisses varied from tender touches to strong searching dances with their tongues. Their two shadows blended into a single, dark, gently swaying image of mutual desire. At least, that's how Erik would have described it. Sheila's depiction would have had a more Anglo-Saxon brevity.

Suddenly, Erik snapped out of his dream. Other shadows were moving toward them at a steady, determined pace. Sheila turned her head and followed his gaze. She froze. In a few seconds, two officers of the *Guardia Civil* confronted them. Each officer held a leather leash. At the other end of each leash was a large German shepherd. Sheila sank against Erik and began to tremble. One of the officers touched his cap, and spoke.

"*Señores, por qué están ustedes aquí? El jardín está cerrado.*" Erik tried to explain in his halting Spanish, but the officer interrupted him in English. "The garden is closed for the night, *señor*. You should not be in here. It is not safe for you. There are sometimes bad men here at night."

"We're sorry, *señor*, we didn't mean any harm," Erik replied.

"Come," said the officer. "We will take you out of here."

The *Guardia Civil* and their canine associates politely escorted Erik and Sheila back to the gate. It was now locked. The officer who had spoken unlocked the gate with a heavy key, then motioned Erik and Sheila outside. The man closed the gate and relocked it from the inside. Touching his hat again, he spoke to them through the iron bars. "*Cuidado, señor.* It is dangerous in the city after dark."

Erik mumbled his thanks, turned, and led Sheila to the car. "Are you okay?" he asked.

"I'm fine."

They drove back to Torremolinos. Erik stopped outside his flat. "You want to stay at my place tonight?"

"What do you want from me?" Sheila whispered.

What *do* I want, he thought. Am I simply playing an egotistical game? Trying to prove to her that I'm different? That I'm not like her father? Erik softly brushed her cheek with the back of his hand. "I'm not sure, Sheila."

She hesitated for a moment, and then grabbed his hand and kissed it. "Okay," she murmured.

They entered Erik's apartment. He lit a candle and put it in the center of his bedside table. Erik put his hands on her shoulders. She was still trembling. "Are you sure you're alright?"

Sheila stared at the floor. "Yes."

"Look," he reassured her, "those guys didn't hurt us. They actually protected us."

"Sure." The candle sputtered. Their shadows wavered on the chalk-white walls.

Erik put his arms around her. "I'm sorry if you were

frightened," he said. "It was my fault. I shouldn't have taken you into the garden when I knew it was closed." He kissed her forehead.

"That's okay."

"I feel bad. I wanted you to have a good time tonight."

She looked up sharply. "I did. I'm fine."

Erik couldn't read her expression in the flickering candlelight. "Maybe I should take you back to your place, see you later in the week," he suggested.

"No! I'm with you tonight." Then she kissed him, hard. She rapidly unbuckled his belt, unzipped his jeans, and began to massage him. It didn't take them long to step out of their clothes.

Sheila rolled onto the bed and pulled Erik down on top of her. She grabbed his hips and plunged him into her body. "I'm giving you my pussy! That's all I have to give."

Erik heard her, but he didn't really understand. He was too surprised at the crude honesty of her language and the roughness of her embrace. A few moments of vigorous thrusts accompanied by Sheila's throaty sighs, and it was over. Erik slowly sank on top of her and laid his head beside her on the pillow.

She stroked his hair and murmured, "You're a beautiful man, a beautiful man."

Erik wanted to keep holding her, to keep seeing her. She was the one to end his loneliness. "And you're a wonderful woman," he whispered.

Sheila hugged him tightly. "Wouldn't it be nice to do this every night? I could move in with you. I like being close to you."

Erik felt a chill. He couldn't respond. The idea frightened him. He didn't want *any* woman to move in with him. Not yet. That would be *too* close. Erik shifted his weight, and lay beside her. "I don't know ... I'm not sure ... I have to think about it," Erik said softly. "We can talk about it in the morning."

Sheila was quiet for a time. "That's okay," she finally said. "You think about it."

Erik fell into a deep sleep.

Now, an hour later, he stood filled with confusion and pain as Sheila glared at him. "Two things I hate most—men and dogs!" Then, without a word, she launched herself at him, her fingernails aimed for his eyes. He caught her by both wrists. The struggle was brief, for something suddenly extinguished within her. The anger seemed to drain from her body. Erik let go of her wrists. She sank down on the bed and buried her face in the pillow. For several seconds she lay absolutely still. Then she screamed into the pillow. A shrill siren shriek that resolved into a dark moan. When Erik tried to take her in his arms and comfort her, she thrashed violently. He backed away and waited. Her moans and sobs slowly lessened. The trembling in her body ceased. Softly, she cried into the pillow. Erik stood next to the bed. He knew better than to touch her now.

She cried for a long time. Finally, her tears subsided. Her fists unclenched, and she released the pillow. Her breathing became deep and regular.

What have I done? Erik thought. Have I treated her just like any other man? Perhaps worse?

Beyond the open window, the surf broke upon the shore, whispered up the beach, and then retreated with a rattle of pebbles in the moonlit foam. Erik left the lights on. He quietly picked up his jeans from the floor, put them on, and buckled his belt carefully. He tiptoed to the kitchen table, took a wooden three-legged stool, and carried it over to the bed. Silently, Erik sat down. He watched over her the rest of the night.

THE DAY YOU LOVE ME

Prologue
She was trapped in a narrow tunnel. Her body was being drawn toward a distant light by some invisible, all-powerful force. Her feet were iron boots, dragging along the tunnel floor. Suddenly something rushed out of the light to sting her, her arm, her cheek, her stomach. The light got closer. She saw an ocean of red and yellow flames. Now the flames were all around her. The hurting thing kept stinging her, made her bleed. A great snake rushed toward her, and the hurting thing was the snake's tongue. It stung her, and snapped back toward a dim figure in the distance. The snake was really a whip, and the figure was whipping her. She knew she was in Hell, and the figure was the Devil. She tried to scream, but no sound came out. Now she was bleeding everywhere,

and the whip was lashing her only on her belly and her bottom and her secret parts in front. Closer and closer she was pulled toward the Devil. She saw the creature's eyes burning brighter than the flames, eyes that stared through her belly at her bad girl's soul. She knew that she was made of sin; that she was about to die, again and again in Hell's flames. Now she stood in front of the Devil, head bowed in shame, staring at the Devil's feet. Something grabbed her chin and slowly made her look up, higher and higher, past the Devil's fiery legs, past the hand and the whip. No! I won't look. I am evil. I deserve to burn in Hell. I won't look. But she couldn't close her eyes. She began to whimper. Again, she tried to scream, and then, eyes wide open, she almost saw the Devil's face.

Sukie Wittmore trembled as she removed the condoms, personal lubricants, and all the sex toys from the drawer of a tiny dresser in the bedroom of her Paris flat on Rue Brea. She dumped these private items in a shoebox, jammed the top back on, and shoved the box beneath her double bed. Her hands shook as she arranged the blanket so it fell nearly to the floor on the side of the bed facing away from the wall. Sukie took a deep breath, and then hastily inspected the rest of the flat to remove any vestige of male presence. Her parents had decided to surprise her with a visit, all the way from Eastfield, Indiana. They would soon be at her door.

Across the street in the Café du Midi to which Sukie had banished him, Ryan Aedan—Sukie's male presence—sat glumly, his hastily stuffed suitcase at his feet. "Don't even dream of coming back till after you see my parents leave," she'd said. "Promise?" The frantic way she'd spoken left little room for argument. But Ryan wanted to protect her. Sukie's parents would try to steal her from him. He wanted to confront them, to smash their mysterious power over her. But he knew that Sukie had to free herself. Ryan looked across Rue Brea at the window of Sukie's apartment. I should have argued anyway, he told himself.

Six months earlier, Ryan had bounced happily down Boulevard du Montparnasse in the soft, late-autumn twilight. Six foot two, slight of build, with dark, curly hair and brown eyes, he was a bundle of enthusiasm. Earlier that afternoon, Charles de Gaulle airport had been the usual seething menagerie in an interminable maze, but Ryan hadn't cared. He was thrilled to be back in Paris. Even the Air France bus to the Gare Montparnasse was a pleasure, as long as he closed his eyes. He knew that most of the one-hour ride was through the steel and concrete wasteland that ringed the old city in a chokehold of hideous 20th century industrial ugliness. As Ryan once described it, the real Paris was surrounded by a malignant incrustation of soulless temples to the all-powerful god of Maximum Profit. The environment be damned. And indeed it was.

But the bus ride was over. Ryan took a deep breath, and flashed a luminous grin. "Thank you, William, as ever, for your good counsel," he murmured. Since high school, Ryan had firmly believed in William Blake's comforting maxim, "The road of excess leads to the palace of wisdom." To Ryan, the palace of wisdom was personified in his image of the ideal woman. But, though his quest was sincere, he wasn't in a hurry to abandon the pleasures of the road.

The atmosphere of freedom in the San Francisco Bay Area had provided the matrix for Ryan's early searches for the elusive palace. Throughout high school and college, he'd entered into each new liaison with an open mind and an untroubled heart. Now, in Paris, he anticipated a lengthy, circuitous route, a road filled with adventures, leading eventually to his *grand amour*. After all, as Blake had added, "You never know what is enough until you know what is more than enough."

As Ryan passed the restaurant La Rotonde, he glanced at the Café Dôme across the Boulevard. He nodded to the ghost of Hemingway and the hundred thousand post-Hemingway phantoms of fledgling writers who had enthusiastically trailed in Hem's wake. Ryan laughed out loud at the image of an endless file of artistic specters floating down the sidewalk and filtering into and out of the venerable—now holy—Café Dôme.

Ryan rounded the corner onto Boulevard Raspail and saluted Rodin's massive sculpture of Balzac. A giant symbol of gargantuan appetite, it had viewed the human comedy from its pedestal amid the trees for well over half a century. Ryan loved the unconventional statue that, naturally, had shocked the general public before and after its current placement.

Though he wasn't delusional, Ryan didn't bother distinguishing real people from fictional characters in Paris history. The Balzac statue prompted images of the writer himself, plus visions of its sculptor Rodin, clumped together with Balzac's characters such as Vautrin, the enigmatic, ruthless criminal genius who was nonetheless capable of overwhelming love, and Rastignac, the ambitious social climber. Ryan visualized them all. Each image had equal importance. Each was an exciting part of the shimmering galaxy of past lives and loves in the ever-alluring, turbulent fantasy called Paris.

Ryan turned left onto the narrow Rue du Montparnasse, and briskly entered the tiny lobby of the two star Hotel des Écrivains, his favorite. At age 26, he'd finished his Ph.D. in history, had some money in the bank, and was now ready to settle for a time in the city of his dreams, the city of romance, the city of women.

After checking in, Ryan took the stairs two at a time up to his tiny room, and threw his suitcase on the narrow bed. He crossed to the small sink, dashed some cold water in his face, and then headed out. The cafe across Raspail looked inviting for an aperitif. As he approached, he noticed Sukie seated alone at a window table, reading the *Herald Tribune*. Ryan liked her look—dark hair, black turtleneck, tight black jeans, black leather boots, and a deep purple silk scarf draped around her neck. Is she Parisian? Maybe British? American?

Ryan glanced through the window at the interior of the Café du Midi. The muted red walls were dotted with brightly colored prints of scenes from the south of France: Matisse, Bonnard, Van Gogh, Cezanne, Picasso, even some of Gauguin's early landscapes that he'd painted around Arles. The vibrant greens and sparkling blues gave the cafe's interior a warm, cheerful ambience. Outside the cafe, a rank of motorcycles and scooters were locked to dull gray steel racks embedded in the cement at the edge of Rue Brea.

He entered the cafe and scanned the room quickly, as if looking for a table or for someone he was supposed to meet. Speed was very important in the game. A quick look, nail the image with a name, and move on. A key element was not to be detected. It wouldn't do to be caught staring at anyone for too long.

Seated at a window table near Sukie was a very thin man of indeterminate age dressed in a green T-shirt, green corduroy jacket and pants, green socks, and bright green shoes. He sat with his back straight, his elbows resting on the table, palms together beneath his chin in a Namaste pose. His eyes were tightly closed. Ryan dubbed him the Praying Mantis.

At a table toward the back were two middle-aged men with dark mustaches and close-cropped hair, each wearing a black leather jacket over a gray T-shirt. One man wore a steel-studded, black leather collar attached to a chain leash held by the other man. They were both laughing and casually sipping their coffee. Jekyll and Hyde.

On a barstool sat a woman with wispy brown hair that escaped in all directions from beneath her red cloche hat. She wore a red blouse and appeared to be drunk. Ryan saw her wobble her nose with her right index finger and, with a boisterous laugh, try to grab the passing waiter's ass. Red Riding Hood.

Near Sukie, at another window table, Ryan noted a solitary, bearded Arab, wearing traditional white headdress, blue jeans, and a wild-west shirt open to the navel. His hairy chest was bedecked with a heavy gold chain. He sipped a glass of mint tea while he read an Arabic newspaper. Ali Baba.

Ryan crossed to Sukie's table and stopped. Yes, of course, Juliette Greco. Sukie looked up. She coolly appraised him for a moment, then went back to her newspaper.

"Excuse me," Ryan said.

Sukie again glanced up from her paper. Since her arrival in Paris, she'd shortened her name—Susanna Katherine—to Sukie, and let her hair grow long. In her black outfit, she was the picture of the Saint Germain *femme fatale*. "Yes? What can I do for you?" she said.

Her cool tone of voice and air of mild irritation almost derailed him. But Ryan had resolved to get to know her. "I don't mean to bother you," he said shyly. Actually, Ryan wasn't shy at all. But he'd discovered that a touch of feigned diffidence increased his charm.

"And?" she said.

"And?"

"What else don't you mean?"

Ryan thought for a moment. He hadn't expected the instant quicksand in this relationship. He decided that a strategic retreat was in order. "Okay. I apologize."

"For what?"

"For bothering you."

"Who said you were bothering me?"

"Well, I certainly got that impression."

"You're not bothering me. But just say what you mean."

"Do you always have a problem with men?"

Sukie blinked. "What do you mean?"

Ryan backed away and raised his hands in a sign of defeat. "I *mean* it's pretty obvious you're busy. Sorry to disturb you." He turned to leave.

"Wait. Just a moment."

"Why?"

"You can sit down."

"Why should I sit down?"

"We could talk."

"I'd be as well off talking to a chain saw."

This made her laugh. "I'm sorry. Was I a bit prickly?"

"That's a euphemism."

"Ooh. Big word."

"This is silly. I'm leaving." Ryan turned and walked toward the door.

"No. Stop."

Ryan stopped, and walked back to her table. "Look, the last thing I expected was to get into a big argument over nothing. This is futile."

"It's not. Please sit down."

Ryan sat down. "I'm making a mistake. I know it."

"Maybe not. I just wanted you to say it."

"Say what?"

"Why you came over to my table."

"You're confusing me."

"No, I'm not. You came over here for the same reason I asked you to sit down, didn't you?"

Ryan laced his hands behind his neck, leaned back, and grinned. "Okay. I suppose so. Any harm in that?"

Sukie smiled. "No. None whatsoever."

The waiter, who had witnessed with amusement their

little dance, now approached the table. "*Voulez-vous boire quelque chose, monsieur?*"

"*Un café, s'il vous plaît.*"

"*Oui, monsieur.*"

As the waiter walked back toward the bar, the man in green suddenly opened his eyes, stood up, and shuffled rapidly over to Sukie's table. He stood beside them, staring at Ryan like a hungry rat examining a shrimp cocktail. Ryan looked up at the man, then back at Sukie. "A friend of yours?"

"Hello, Green," Sukie said in a bored tone of voice. "Don't worry about him," she told Ryan. "He doesn't bite."

This did not reassure Ryan. "I see," he said, and fell silent.

Sukie appeared undisturbed by Green's presence. "So, we were talking about why you stopped over to see me," she said cheerfully.

Ryan glanced up again at Green. "Hmmm. Well, probably because you look like Juliette Greco."

"Who is she?"

"She's a singer who was called the darling of the Existentialists, *la muse de Saint-Germain-des-Prés*. She has a low, sexy voice, gentle brown eyes, often wears all black, and she looks and sounds smart. I fell in love with her when I was a high school freshman studying French. My dad has many of her records. I loved one particular song about the night, Juliette asking the night to bring her a lover, *un amant*."

Sukie looked Ryan in the eye. "Not an unreasonable request."

"No. Certainly not."

Suddenly Green leaned down, stared into Ryan's face, and bleated, "What's that got to do with hamsters?"

Before Ryan could formulate an appropriate response, Green spun on his heels, shuffled back to his own table, and resumed his meditative pose.

Ryan looked at Sukie. "So you know the Praying Mantis?"

"The what?"

"The Praying Mantis. It's a game I play. I check out the tables in a cafe, and I give a nickname to anyone who looks interesting. It helps me remember them."

"Sounds like fun. Actually, I just call him Green. The story goes that somewhere near Mumbai, Green marinated his brain in a soup of amphetamines, opium derivatives, and other magic potions. He somehow got back here to Paris. How or where he lives, nobody knows. But we see him everywhere on the Left Bank, at all hours of the day or night. He's ubiquitous."

"Sad story," Ryan mused.

"Do I have a nickname?"

"Yes. I already told you."

Sukie caught the reference and smiled. "So, back to Juliette Greco's *amant*."

"What about him?"

"You said you love the song. Tell me about it."

"Well, I used to go to sleep wishing that I were that lover. But I was too young, and I figured she'd laugh at me, pat me on the head, and tell me to come back and see her when I was a bit older. I felt this great desire for her and, at the same time, a kind of humiliation, as if I'd actually been rejected. Anyway, as I grew up, I'm sure my subconscious dedicated all my wet dreams to her."

"Sounds like an interesting woman."

"She is. But back to you. What's your real name?"

"Sukie."

"Mine's Ryan."

"Hi, Ryan."

"Hi. Now, Sukie, why *were* you so prickly?"

Sukie raised her eyebrows. "I had a really weird childhood."

"Doesn't everyone?"

"Not like mine. For example, when I was a sophomore in high school, my parents got my biology teacher in trouble because he used the word 'vagina' in class."

"Vagina. Ooh, that's almost as bad as teaching evolution."

"Yeah, isn't it. Well, anyway, our textbook lesson was on reproduction, and the word was in the book. Mom heard about the class from a friend in church. Mother dear then went storming into the principal's office and accused my teacher of leading a nasty discussion about a woman's private parts."

"What happened to the teacher?"

"He got hauled in front of the professional standards inquisition. Fortunately, he brought the textbook with him, so he got off with a warning. This made my parents furious. They wanted him fired."

Ryan shook his head. He chose his words with care. Satirical depiction was one thing, blunt criticism another. "I guess I ... just can't understand your parents' point of view."

"Don't even try. But know that it exists."

Just then, an elderly man with a white beard flowing

from his cheeks halfway down to his waist entered the cafe. He carried a bandoneon, the small accordion-like instrument that is the classic soul of tango music. Ryan watched with delight as the man slowly settled himself at a table near the bar. "It looks like Walt Whitman's going to play us a tango."

"How do you know? He hasn't started yet."

"You'll see. Just listen."

The waiter, who seemed to know the man, smiled and brought him a small glass of beer. The Whitmanesque musician took a few sips, set the glass on the table, and closed his eyes. He began to play a slow, melancholy tango.

"See, I told you," Ryan whispered. "This is one of Carlos Gardel's most famous tunes: *El Dia Que Me Quieras*, The Day You Love Me."

"It's beautiful."

Sukie and Ryan listened quietly as the man played. When the tune was over, the people in the cafe applauded. The musician played another tango, this one more up-tempo than the Gardel piece. Then he finished his beer in a gulp, and walked from table to table, collecting coins from his audience.

"Do you like music, Sukie?"

"Sure. I love music."

"My dad has a huge music library. I grew up listening to all kinds of music. How about dancing, do you like to dance?"

"Of course. But I don't know how to tango. Do you?"

Ryan grinned. "No, I'm afraid not. I just like the music." He was silent for a moment, and then glanced at his watch. "What are you doing for dinner tonight?"

They strolled down Rue Brea toward the darkened Jardin du Luxembourg.

"So, Sukie, tell me more about your strange childhood."

"I was an only child. Guess my parents figured I was enough."

Ryan sometimes had to lean close to hear Sukie's soft voice through the roar of passing motorcycles, so close to her that he could smell her perfume amidst the ever-present exhaust fumes. He made a mental note to find out what scent she was wearing.

They turned down Rue Vavin, crossed Rue Guynemer, and looped around the park to Rue Vaugirard. As they walked, Ryan learned a lot more about Sukie's family life. Her father was a proctologist and her mother a devoted horsewoman. They were ardent members of a very strict Protestant church, whose rigid doctrine specified that any person who had ever lived, was now living, or who might live in the future was eternally damned to a literal hell, complete with literal fire and menacing pitchforks, if said persons were not members of her parents' enlightened sect. If anyone outside the one true faith questioned this subtle theological point, Sukie's mother would shut them up with a cheerfully condescending "Well, it's your choice."

Sukie grimaced. "According to my parents, there are only two options. Each confused heretic can join the church or face the music."

As they crossed Vaugirard to the Place de l'Odéon, Ryan idly wondered how Christ, Buddha, Gandhi, Mother Teresa, and so many others had managed to fall so deeply into the black Chasm of Error. "Fortunately, I was spared the plague of religion when I grew up," Ryan said. "My parents were devout pagans."

"You're lucky," said Sukie. "And I'm sure your parents let you have girlfriends."

Ryan was puzzled. "Of course they did. Why wouldn't they?"

"Good question. In my family, boyfriends were

definitely out. My parents controlled everything I did. And they made me feel guilty about everything, even the clothes I wanted to wear. I used to get these weird nightmares, but since I've been here, they've gone away."

"I guess I was lucky to grow up in a pretty liberal family."

Ryan's parents' beliefs were rooted in the austere, romantic ideas of the Existentialism of post-war France. Such phrases as "existence precedes essence" had been in Ryan's mind since early childhood. He shared his parents' belief that our every conscious moment presents us with choices. We have the freedom to define ourselves, and the corresponding responsibility. If we screw up our lives by our own actions, it's our own fault. But the idea of choice meant something very different to Ryan than it did to Sukie's parents.

Ryan and Sukie walked past the Thèatre de l'Odéon. The majestic pillars cast deep shadows in the moonlight.

"I love this building," Sukie exclaimed. "It looks more like an old temple than a theater."

"That's not a surprise. The name Odéon comes from ancient Roman and Greek buildings used for poetry contests, music, even musical theater productions."

"I know," Sukie said. "The name's based on a Greek word that means song."

"How do you know that?"

Sukie gave Ryan a wry smile. "I thought it was common knowledge."

"Oh. Of course."

They meandered down the Rue de l'Odéon toward the Boulevard Saint Germain, heading for the bustling Carrefour de l'Odéon with its galaxy of busy cafes, movie theaters, magazine stands, postcard racks, liquor shops, wine bars, kiosks with giant posters blaring news headlines, myriad motorcycles, scooters, and bicycles chained to dark iron poles planted at the edge of the sidewalk. The sounds of ten thousand footsteps mingled with the bellow of passing buses. A stream of people erupted from the underground metro stop and flowed into the Carrefour delta.

As Ryan and Sukie approached the intersection, the cars on Saint Germain grudgingly stopped when the light turned red. Engines roaring, headlights blazing, exhausts belching, the cars impatiently waited, loading the air with greasy fumes, an endless pack of ravening, panting, steel dogs, straining at an invisible gate, ready to leap ahead at the earliest possible second until—tires squealing, engines howling—they would roar off in tight formation along the street until the pack was again halted, brakes screeching angrily, at the next red light.

"Paris would be so much nicer without the cars," Ryan said. "Trust the spiritually stunted, aesthetically numb city planners to let such beautiful streets become polluted racetracks, and even turn the banks of the Seine into goddam freeways!"

Sukie laughed. "So how do you really feel about that?"

"Was I preaching? Sorry."

"That's all right. I agree, though I've never quite phrased it your way."

They reached the opposite sidewalk unscathed just as the stoplight changed. "Are you tired? Do you mind walking a bit more?" Ryan asked.

"Not at all. I like walking."

"I know a great little place a few blocks from here. The area's very touristic, but the restaurant's a good one."

Sukie took his arm. "Let's go."

The restaurant Chez Mireille fronted a tiny side street off Rue St. André des Arts. Sukie peered into the dimly lit interior and saw a dozen or so tables, each with a white tablecloth and a white taper in a simple silver candleholder.

The tuxedo-clad maitre'd ushered the pair down a flight of stone stairs into a cave with limestone walls lit at intervals by dimly glowing sconces. He seated them at a corner table. The far wall was a group of tinted glass panels with a swinging glass door in the center. Beyond the glass lay a dark, floor-to-ceiling wine cellar. "I'm impressed, "Sukie said. "This is a beautiful place."

"Don't your other boyfriends take you to nice restaurants?"

Sukie appeared not to notice the word *other* in Ryan's question. "Some did, but it's been a while since I've had any boyfriends."

Ryan welcomed this bit of information. "No boyfriends? I thought you were a free spirit living the high life in swinging Paris."

"Are you mocking me?"

"No. I'm just trying to get to know you better."

"Sure, I've had some boyfriends. But they just drifted away, or perhaps I'm the one who drifted. I haven't met anyone all that interesting."

More good news to Ryan. The waiter brought the menus. "If you like fish, I recommend the poached salmon," Ryan said.

Sukie folded her menu and replaced it on the table. "Whatever you suggest." She glanced around the room, admiring the ancient stone walls and the romantic ambience. "This is beautiful. I love having dinner by candlelight, even when I'm alone in my apartment."

"You do? Even when you're alone?"

"Yes. It's so different from the way I grew up. My parents and I would sit at a white Formica-topped table, stuffing our faces in a brightly lit kitchen while they watched reruns of old sitcoms on a small TV set."

"That's not dining. That's a feeding."

Sukie tilted her head slightly, looked intensely at Ryan, and gave a slow, gentle smile.

"You're so beautiful when you smile," Ryan blurted out, then caught himself. He was afraid he'd revealed himself too soon—the perfect setup for rejection by a woman who doesn't want to be tied down to some sentimental attachment. *You heard her*, he told himself, *no boyfriends for a while. Maybe she was just bored this afternoon. So I come along, and she thinks if this guy wants to take me out to dinner, fine. Better than sitting at home with a book. But why should her opinion matter to me? I just got here. Tomorrow's another day, right?*

The waiter reappeared. Ryan tried to conceal his

worry and his anger at himself as he ordered the dinners and a bottle of St. Veran. As the waiter walked back toward the stone stairs, Ryan sat in silence, focusing on the wine cellar at the end of the room. *So now what? A chatty meal, take her back to her flat, she thanks me for a nice evening, I had a good time, she'll say, and she hopes I enjoy my stay in Paris, perhaps we'll see each other again, someday, and she's sorry, but her calendar is filled up for the next six months, so—*

"Ryan?" Sukie said softly.

"What?"

"Are you alright?"

"Oh. Was I being rude? Just off in my own world, I guess."

"Did you understand me? That I don't have any other boyfriends?"

Is she just being kind to me, trying to let me down easy, not wanting to bruise my fragile ego? Sure, he's nice enough, she maybe thinks, but too much emotion isn't worth the trouble. And why the hell should I care? She's not the first woman I've taken out to dinner.

"Ryan? Say something."

"I guess I understand. I'm not sure."

"Please, be sure."

Back to you, Ryan. And don't be a jerk. Listen to

what she's saying. Look at her. She's not dismissing you as some sappy sentimentalist. Now's not the time for a stupid display of adolescent defensiveness. "Okay. I'm sure."

"Good. And thank you for saying you like it when I smile."

The waiter brought the wine and deftly poured a touch in Ryan's glass. "*Monsieur?*"

Ryan briefly examined the color then handed the glass to Sukie. "You be the official taster."

Sukie took a sip. "Excellent," and she handed the glass back to Ryan.

"I trust your judgment," he said, and nodded to the waiter. "So. Sukie. You've been here a while. How's your French?"

"Basic. But getting better. How's yours?"

"Also basic. I studied it in high school and college, but I can't claim to feel comfortable yet. What was your major?"

"English lit, with a minor in Romance languages."

Ryan grinned. "Did that include Romance Greek?"

"Oh, you mean the Odéon. I confess. I looked it up one day after I walked by the theater. And you? What did you study?"

"History." Ryan saw no reason to mention any advanced degrees. Not good to seem too impressed with one's own academic credentials.

Dinner was presented. Sukie was right. The wine was excellent.

They dined in a leisurely fashion. Much of their conversation involved a comparison between growing up in San Francisco and Sukie's life in her small town in Indiana.

Both Ryan and Sukie were delighted to find in the other an enthusiasm for other cultures, other ways of life. "I wish everyone felt that way," Sukie said. "How can anyone actually believe that *their* opinions are the only valid ones, that their own way of life is the universal standard against which to measure the shortcomings of the rest of humanity!"

"A good question. I agree. Though I've never quite phrased it your way."

"Touché. My turn to preach."

"That's okay. I like it when you get excited." The waiter brought the dessert menu. "Would you like a glass of Sauternes with dessert?" Ryan asked. "It goes well with the *tarte Tatin*."

"That sounds perfect."

And of course, it was.

Ryan ordered each of them an espresso. As they

finished their coffee, Sukie was surprised to realize they were the last customers in that part of the restaurant. The upstairs was equally quiet. We've been talking for hours, she thought. How rare. How nice.

They walked back through the darkened Buci market, turned up Rue de Seine, and then strolled down St. Germain toward the church. As they passed Les Deux Magots cafe, Ryan gave an obligatory salute to the ghosts of Sartre and Simone de Beauvoir. He used his left hand because his right was firmly resting on Sukie's slim waist. They crossed St. Germain and caught a cab at the taxi stand near the Brasserie Lipp.

Ryan and Sukie sat quietly as the driver accelerated up Rue de Rennes and aimed his vehicle at Boulevard Raspail. At least he's not mauling me in the backseat of the taxi, Sukie thought, though I'm not sure I'd mind if he did. And when we arrive at my apartment? Of course, he'll want to come in and stay the night. And in the morning, he'll buy me breakfast, and tell me he really wants to see me again. He'll be busy for a time looking for some kind of job, but maybe, in a few weeks, we could meet again at the Midi, get a pizza or something, and then back to my place. Pretty soon, one of us will just drift away.

The taxi stopped. Ryan paid the driver, and then walked Sukie up to the door of her building. To her surprise, he merely gave her a chaste kiss on the cheek. "Are you busy tomorrow, Sukie?"

"No."

"Shall we have lunch? The Place de la Contrescarpe is always interesting. I'll pick you up around noon."

"I haven't said yes—yet."

"Oh. I guess I got a bit ahead of myself."

Sukie lightly brushed Ryan's lips with a kiss. "See you at noon," she whispered.

Ryan walked slowly back toward his hotel. He was deeply puzzled. All he could think about was seeing Sukie again. What a strange evening, he thought. She's fascinating. She even likes history. Amazing. This is new. I've never felt so in tune with someone before. All evening, not one second of boredom, not one bit of extra effort needed to keep the conversation going. But slow down, Ryan. You just got here. It must be the newness of the situation, my own imagination plus the charge I always get when I return to Paris. Would I feel this way if I'd met her in San Francisco? But what did Balzac say? In Paris, reality attains a degree of coincidence that is far greater than any writer could invent. Something like that. And he's right. This is certainly not what I expected my first day back here.

Ryan realized he was much too wound up to go back to the emptiness of his hotel room. He wandered down Boulevard du Montparnasse. The Bar Select was still open. He went in, stood at the bar, and ordered a cognac.

A tall African man standing on Ryan's right was enjoying a large glass of beer, apparently one of many, for the man had beer running down his chin. Several large wet patches decorated the front of his red and yellow striped, ankle-length robe. Suddenly, the man lurched, bumped into Ryan's shoulder, and sloshed some more beer on himself. "*Oh, oh, pardon.*" The man's broad smile revealed that his few remaining teeth were a distressing combination of yellow and black. "*Encore, pardon, mon ami,*" he muttered as he tried to focus his eyes, which were shot through with red streaks like a map of central Paris. With an unsteady hand, he held out his glass toward Ryan. "*Tu veux partager?*"

"*Merci.* I have cognac."

"English? You want?"

"No, thank you."

But the man was determined. "I share, you drink, good beer."

"Thanks, but I prefer my own drink." Ryan pointed to his cognac and turned his back on the man.

As the beer drinker wove through the crowd looking for another friend to share with, a short, plump fellow on Ryan's left nodded his head and smiled. He was dressed in a dark blue suit and a light blue cravat, and wore three gold rings on his right hand. "You must be careful in this district at this hour," the man warned. "And of your friends. That man is a thief. Everyone here knows him."

Ryan noted the speaker's accent was French. "Thanks for the tip."

The man sipped his champagne. "This is your first time in Paris?"

"No, I've been here several times before. And I'm happy to be back."

"When did you arrive?"

"Just today."

"Oh, well then, perhaps you haven't had time to find a suitable hotel? I have a very nice apartment close by. You're welcome to spend the night."

"No thanks, I've got a place. But you're very nice to offer."

Ryan finished his drink, nodded politely to the gentleman, and decided to go back to his hotel room, and no doubt dream of Sukie.

The following afternoon, Ryan and Sukie picked an outdoor table in the shade across from the famous Brasserie La Chope. Now, they both played the game, scanning the people at the other tables.

To their left, a woman in her early twenties was holding an animated conversation with the waiter. She wore a chic, very clinging beige silk blouse, tight-fitting black pants, and black four-inch heels. Her gold bangles glinted and clicked on her arm as she emphasized important points in the discussion of the menu. As Ryan was admiring her stylish, thick blond hair, the woman turned and glanced in his direction. To his surprise, he saw that the hitherto obscured side of her head was shaved bald, and a red and green fire-breathing dragon was painted on her scalp. "Lizard Lady," Ryan pronounced.

"That's an easy one," Sukie whispered.

Near Lizard Lady sat a handsome, turbaned and bearded Sikh whose liquid brown eyes were staring soulfully into the vacant blue orbs of a mesmerized, scruffy teenage girl wearing a Mexican *serape* draped over her shoulders and falling to the knees of her artfully torn jeans.

"Houdini and friend," Sukie offered.

"Not perfect, but it'll do."

To the right of Ryan and Sukie, two male skinheads, arms, necks, and scalps garishly tattooed, sported black leather vests open to reveal a galaxy of other menacing tattoos on their chests. They were talking loudly in English to a young woman sitting between them. She had a pink Mohawk, chartreuse shorts, black army boots with the laces untied, and a variety of piercings in her nose, ears, and eyebrows. One of her companions had the phrase 'fuck off!' tattooed on his forearm. Each man groped the girl's nearest thigh with one hand, while his other hand gripped a massive glass tankard of beer.

"The Three Graces," Ryan declared.

"No argument."

At the next table, shielded by a tightly buttoned-up white raincoat, was a wizened, gray-haired lady wearing round, coke-bottle glasses. She sipped a glass of red wine, and from her salad speared tiny bits of lettuce, which she chewed on abstractedly with her front teeth as she read an English language guidebook.

"The Woman in White?" Ryan suggested.

"No, that's too obvious. Look at her nibble. How about the White Rabbit?"

"Perfect."

The waiter approached their table. Ryan and Sukie

ordered a *poulet rôti, pommes frites* and a simple white burgundy. The waiter promptly brought the wine, opened the bottle, and unceremoniously plunked it into the ice bucket on their table.

"I've got passes to the Louvre today," Ryan said as he poured their wine. "This way we don't have to stand in line."

"You won't believe it, but I've never been to the Louvre."

"Well, it's always crowded, but it's still fascinating."

As Ryan raised his glass to toast Sukie, he was alarmed to see a tall, spindly figure clad entirely in green shuffling across the square toward their cafe. "Oh no. Is this really happening?"

Sukie laughed. "I told you he was ubiquitous."

Green appeared not to notice them, and sat down at a front table right next to the pavement.

Two men with tattered clothes and long hair matted with dirt lounged on the tiny patch of grass at the center of the square. Occasionally, each would knock back a mouthful of red wine from a large plastic bottle. They shared a cigarette.

"I've noticed quite a few homeless people in Paris this time," Ryan said. "Every time I come here, it seems there are more."

"Yes, from all over the EU, I guess."

"I'd hate to be in their position."

"So would I."

The waiter arrived with the lunches and poured the couple more wine. "*Vous désirez autre chose, Monsieur?*"

"*Non, merci.*"

Ryan looked at the plates with approval. "I like this place."

"Yes, I like it too. I like almost all of Paris. I'm going to stay here for a long time."

"Me too. I even have a job here, if I want it. A part-time bartender and waiter."

"How's that? I thought only EU citizens could work legally."

"Who said it was legal? I've got a friend who owns a so-called American restaurant, complete with saddles on posts for barstools, and bleached skulls with horns decorating the walls. It's out in Clichy."

"Saddles? Cattle bones and horns? That's the French image of an American restaurant?"

"The cowboy image dies hard. Last summer, I was walking down Saint Germain, and a waiter came running out of a restaurant and offered me a couple packets of sugar."

"Why?"

"That's exactly what I asked him. Very deadpan, he said it was for my horse."

"Very funny."

"How about you, Sukie? Did you find any work here?"

"Actually, yes. Like you, it's probably not legal, but I'm a part-time English tutor for the children of a few wealthy Parisians."

Suddenly, Green materialized next to their table, and fixed Ryan with a beady stare. "Hello, Green," Ryan said with resignation.

"It's all well and good, until the dog dies," Green peeped. He nodded sagely, and then vanished into the dim interior of the brasserie.

"Green seems to like you," Sukie said.

"I'm guess I'm honored."

Just then, one of the homeless men out in the square lurched to his feet and brandished an empty plastic bottle. "Ve ahr shadows!" he announced, as he made his way across the pavement to the cafe tables, one rough, calloused hand held out for contributions. "Ve ahr illusions. Blood spots in desert ov bones."

Ryan was surprised to hear the man speaking English and couldn't quite place the accent. Romanian? As the man approached their table, Ryan noted that his eyes—though bleary with alcohol—had a wild, penetrating, intelligent look. An Old Testament prophet, Ryan thought. "Jeremiah," Ryan whispered to Sukie.

The man stopped directly in front of Sukie, and leaned toward her. "Bevare temptation," he growled. Although Ryan was annoyed at the intrusion, he gave the man a few coins and waved him away. Ryan watched the man drift off to other tables.

"That was generous," Sukie said, trembling slightly.

"Yeah. He's obviously drunk, and yet when I see guys like that, I always wonder what their story is." Ryan looked at Sukie. "What's the matter?"

"It's nothing. Something about him reminded me of my father."

"Your father likes cheap wine?"

"No, he doesn't drink." Sukie took a deep breath. "Look, you got the dinner. Let me get the lunch."

Sukie paid the bill. Hand in hand, they headed back down Rue Descartes toward the Louvre.

As Ryan and Sukie wove through the packed museum crowd, they spotted an English language tour and followed it into the next room. They stood still at the back of the group, holding hands, and listened to the female guide's explication of a sumptuous nude called *La Grande Odalisque*.

"This next painting was commissioned by Napoleon's sister and painted by Ingres while he was living in Italy. The works of Ingres during this period clearly bear witness to their voluptuous objecthood, and they require the viewer to focus on a consentient center that is topographically unavoidable. This painting coalesces in a sensual harmony that is almost unspeakably organic. We see a universal feminine cosmic force field, an ontological synergism, where the slightest perturbation could result in a ripple of endless carnal consequence."

Ryan and Sukie exchanged a glance. Sukie gave Ryan's hand a little squeeze. "Is she saying what I think she's saying?"

"That the Odalisque has a memorable ass?"

Sukie stifled a laugh. "Yes."

"I think you're right." They contained their laughter as the guide continued.

"Though the painting's fleshly accessibility defies strictly linear explication, the superlative interaction between succulent non-rationalized masses and gestural ambiguity is more than subliminally stimulating. It's all there." A beatific smile suffused the face of the enraptured guide. "Are there any questions?"

Ryan took this opportunity to lead Sukie into the next room, ahead of the tour group. He looked at Sukie. "Well, that was enlightening."

She looked back at Ryan. Suddenly, Sukie doubled over and spun around, eyes wide, laughing hysterically. "I can hardly breathe," she said.

Then Ryan began to laugh. They laughed till tears streamed down their cheeks. They looked at each other again, and again burst into a fit of laughter. And it was during that second look that Ryan gave up all resistance. He knew that he was completely in love with Sukie. She was the one. His *grand amour* in the flesh. He could not let her go.

Eventually, their laughter subsided. "You want to see something else funny?" Ryan asked.

"Sure, but the tour guide's speech will be hard to beat."

"This is more physical humor. Actually, almost slapstick."

"Okay. Lead on."

"You asked for it. Off we go to the Mona Lisa."

Ryan steered them through the seething mob toward the thirteenth to fifteenth century Italian painting section. "Did you bring your binoculars?" Ryan asked. They reached the edge of a densely packed horde of art lovers who were politely elbowing and shoving one another to get nearer to a small painting that hung behind a bullet-proof glass shield in the distance. Ryan pointed toward the painting over the heads of the surging crowd. "There it is. Now you've seen it." And he pulled her away from the undulating mass of sweating humanity.

"A breathtaking spectacle," Sukie said.

"This place supposedly gets about 10 million visitors a year, and it's closed on Tuesdays and a few holidays. You want a rough average of the daily onslaught? Do the math. Divide 10 million by 310 days, although that's not bothering to factor in the denser mob when entrance is free on the first Sunday of each month and on July 14."

"I suppose you know the answer."

"By my calculations, it's over 32,000 people a day, packed inside during the nine-hour period when the museum is regularly open."

"Unbelievable."

"The best thing to do here is to look for any area where the crowds aren't, and you'll always turn up something interesting."

They wandered through the building, casually waving at the Venus de Milo and the Winged Victory, each dimly visible over the heads of the mob of tourists. On rare occasions, they found an area where they could actually approach an artwork without being shoved aside by their fellow aesthetes.

Toward the 6 p.m. closing time, the couple joined the ant-like procession that the guards shepherded toward the exits. They strolled slowly past the Place du Carrousel, then turned left onto the Pont Royale. At the center of the span, they stopped to watch the Bateaux Mouches glide beneath the bridges in the early twilight. The massive, barge-like boats of glass and steel, spotlights lining the railings, cast a shifting, ghostly glare on the buildings along the river. The dinner cruises had started. Live music—violin, piano, accordion—echoed off the cement walls bordering the Seine.

"Sukie?"

"Yes?"

"What happened at Contrescarpe today? I mean with you and our drunken Jeremiah? You were really scared."

"Jeremiah. A good name. You worship false gods, you get destruction, pain, exile."

"You said he reminded you of your father."

"And my mother, if that's possible. Let's walk."

"Sure. We'll go back toward Saint Michel and have a glass of wine."

They turned left along the Quai Voltaire and slowly walked along the river.

"It's complicated. I told you my parents were fierce churchgoers. Well, when I was a young girl, they enrolled me as a day student in an exclusive girls' boarding school. My teachers were strict Puritans, very strict."

"Did you wear uniforms?"

"No. My teachers said only the Catholics wore uniforms. So my mother bought my clothes, and my dad had to approve everything I wore. As a little kid, I was kind of excited to be able to show off to Daddy."

"But as you got older?"

"Things changed. Maybe I was an early developer. I don't know, but each day, my parents got more and more critical."

Ryan listened in silence as Sukie told him about her early teenage years. She had felt deeply humiliated at every mandatory fashion show whenever she saw the telltale frown on either parent's face. "Don't want our baby girl looking like a Jezebel," her father would say. "We are doing God's will, teaching you the ways of

Godliness," her mother would add. They made Sukie return all unacceptable attire. "It's for your own good. We're only protecting you because we love you," was her parents' chorus.

Sukie had been mortified when a clerk occasionally asked her what was wrong with the garments. "By the time I was 15, almost nothing was acceptable. Whenever I started to object, my mother told me never to argue with my father. If I did, he wouldn't love me anymore." At first, Sukie had felt guilty about being angry. But soon the guilt turned into a suppressed rage at both of them.

Ryan and Sukie had a late dinner at a Greek restaurant near Place St. Michel, and lingered over coffee to listen to the bouzouki player. It was long after midnight when, once again, they were at Sukie's door. Ryan hesitated. What's the problem? he thought. You're acting like a junior high school boy on his first date. At least, say something. "What kind of perfume do you wear?"

"Chanel No. 5."

"Ah. A classic. I like it."

"Thank you."

This is silly. Kiss her. Ryan put both hands on Sukie's

waist. Sukie tilted her head back and looked up at him. Ryan dropped both hands to his sides. "Well, I … it's just that … I really had a good time yesterday … and today." Ryan, stop being such a dolt! What do you mean you only had a good time? You were ecstatic. It was magic. So tell her. "What I mean is—"

Without a word, Sukie reached out, took his hands in hers, and replaced them on her hips. "Just say what you mean."

"I mean I love … being with you. And I don't want to leave."

"Then don't," she murmured, just before he kissed her.

The next day, Ryan checked out of his hotel and moved in with Sukie. He was happy in the simply furnished apartment. At one end of the living/dining room was a black leather couch. In front of the couch sat a wrought iron, glass-topped coffee table. Next to the window facing Rue Brea was a sturdy, wooden dining table with two chairs. Against the wall opposite the window stood a tall, dark-walnut bookcase filled with paperbacks. Sukie's CD player was placed on the top shelf.

The small kitchen was separated from the main room by a white-tiled counter. The bathroom was off the kitchen, and the bedroom was off the bathroom. One had to pass through the kitchen and the bathroom to reach the bedroom.

Winter in Paris is cold, wet, and dark, but never dreary. At least not for Ryan and Sukie. Ryan did get his restaurant job, and Sukie acquired a few more students, enough to keep her busy. After work, the pair would meet in the Café du Midi and eagerly discuss the day's happenings. They shared the rent, the cooking and cleaning, the grocery shopping, and Sukie's comfortable double bed. In the evenings, they went to movies, concerts in dark churches, lectures, and occasionally the theater. They spent hours exploring the multitude of cafes and museums—avoiding the Louvre—throughout the city. On rare occasions, they went to restaurants. It was cheaper and much more fun to cook at home.

Ryan accumulated a small music library that, of course, included tunes by Juliette Greco and Carlos Gardel. Often, after dining at home by candlelight, the couple spent a long time dancing slowly together around the living room, and then retiring to the bedroom. Neither of them had ever been so happy.

Yet there were shadows. Sukie hadn't told Ryan everything about her family life. And after Ryan moved in, she'd pretty much dropped the subject. Over a period of months, Ryan had merely learned that her grossly overweight father had practiced medicine for less than a year before lapsing back into the inert bliss of living off the lavish income his grandfather had provided for him. As far as Ryan knew, Sukie's mother—a caustic, skinny nonentity, according to Sukie—was nothing but a distant echo of her father, supporting all his opinions, and frowning on cue at everything Sukie had done or wanted to do or even suggested she might do. For example, Sukie had wanted to go away to a university on the East Coast, but her parents had insisted that she go to a nearby Christian college and live at home. They'd refused to pay for anything else. Sukie strongly resented this. Ryan nicknamed her parents Botero and Giacometti, a blimp and a beanpole.

Ryan knew nothing about Sukie's own small, education trust fund, ironically set up for her by her parents when she was a young child. At 21, when Sukie graduated from college, she also got control of the remnants of the education fund, enough to sustain her for many months while she found an income source of her own. So, the day after graduation, she had asked her parents if it would be okay for her to spend a year in Paris, just that final bit of polish, you know, improve her

French. It would do her good before she returned home to seek a suitable husband chosen, of course, from the Church congregation. The subtext of her "request" was not lost on her parents—they couldn't stop her. Her father had merely frowned and cast a meaningful look at a silver ring on the little finger of Sukie's left hand.

One afternoon, Ryan came home early and found Sukie lying on the couch, staring at the ceiling. Her hands were cold to his touch. "Sukie, what's wrong?" She didn't seem to hear him. She just kept looking up at nothing, at least nothing Ryan could see. "Please tell me what's wrong, Sukie. Did I do something?"

"Nothing's wrong. Just another phone call from my parents."

Another phone call. "How often do they call you?"

"Once or twice a month, early afternoon, you're always at work."

"Is that the problem? Your parents' phone call?" Ryan carefully pulled her off the couch and hugged her tightly. They stood together for a long time in the quiet living room, Sukie as rigid as an icicle.

Eventually, she began to relax, and put her arms around him. "Let's go get coffee," she said. "I want to get outside where I can breathe again." Once out in the street, Sukie seemed to regain her normal mood. "It's nothing," she told Ryan. "I just don't like my parents checking up on me. I'm old enough to live my own life. And it's *my* life I want, not theirs."

That night after they made love, Ryan flashed a mischievous grin and lightly jostled Sukie, who was about to fall asleep. "Have you ever used toys?"

"Toys?" Sukie said drowsily.

"You know, sex toys. "

Sukie thought for a moment. "No. I guess I haven't. Have you?"

"Not really, but I've always been curious. Could we try some?"

"Sure, if you want to."

"It could be fun."

"Maybe … "

"I'll get some tomorrow."

The following afternoon, Ryan stopped in a sex shop and purchased an array of novelty items that he brought home in a plastic grocery bag. For the next few weeks, he and Sukie experimented. It was fun, playful, sometimes even pleasurable. But after a few weeks more, the items tended to remain undisturbed in one of Sukie's dresser drawers. They simply weren't necessary.

Winter blended into spring. The Paris April was cold and wet. The mornings usually began with a clear blue sky and bright sunshine. But often, in a short time, dark clouds would cover the city and unleash a torrent of rain. Huge drops splashed off the cars and the pavement. The wind swirled and pushed the rain in every direction, sending the pedestrians scurrying into cafes, doorways, stores, whatever shelter was at hand. Umbrellas were useless.

On a particularly blustery afternoon in mid-April, Ryan dashed under the awning at the entrance to the Midi, shook the water off his raincoat, and entered the warm cafe. His favorite table wasn't occupied. A very favorable sign. He and Sukie had great plans for the evening: first, an early snack at the cafe, then a production of one of Corneille's classics at the Odéon, and finally a late dinner at the lively Brasserie Balzar. It was their six-month anniversary; Ryan couldn't wait for Sukie to join him. Soon, he spotted her running up Raspail from the Notre-Dame-des-Champs metro station. He hopped up to greet her at the door and embraced her, wet raincoat and all.

They ordered *croque monsieurs* and a *pichet* of Côtes du Rhône, and launched into a discussion of their day and their plans for the evening. After coffee, they crossed Rue Brea to the flat to change clothes.

As they were about to leave for the theater, Sukie's phone rang. "Let them leave a message," Ryan urged. "We don't want to be late for the play."

But Sukie had already answered. "Hello?" Sukie stood absolutely still for a moment, and then turned to look at Ryan, her face a tragic mask.

Oh, no, someone's died, thought Ryan. He moved swiftly toward Sukie to be ready to comfort her. Sukie stopped him with a brusque gesture, put her finger to her lips, and pleaded with her eyes for him to be silent, to not make a sound. Ryan was alarmed to see her begin to shake.

"Okay, sure," Sukie answered softly. "Yes, of course … when will you be here? Around 5 p.m. tomorrow. Sure … you have my address. Okay. What do you mean, why am I so quiet? I'm surprised, that's all. Okay, okay. See you then."

The planned post-theater dinner at the Balzar was not

the joyful affair either Ryan or Sukie had envisioned.

"I don't want you to meet them," she said.

"Why not?"

"I already told you. My Dad forbids me to have boyfriends."

"Sounds to me like your dad has some unresolved reverse-Oedipal issues."

"What?"

"You know, rather than his mother, he wants his little girl all to himself."

Sukie shuddered. "Don't joke about that."

"Maybe I'm only half joking."

"I don't care. Don't even think about that."

"Okay. Sorry." Sukie just grunted. "So what time do they arrive?" Ryan asked.

"They said around five. You'll have to hang out across the street tomorrow afternoon. And you must take all your things out of the apartment."

"So you really refuse to introduce me?"

"And have them give both of us the third degree?"

"I can take it."

Sukie reached over and took Ryan's hand. "Please, Ryan. Please understand. This is something I have to handle alone. They'll only be here for a few days."

That night, Ryan climbed into bed and stretched out beside Sukie. He leaned over to kiss her. As his kisses became more intense, she pushed him away. "No. No, I can't. Not tonight."

"What's wrong? Is it because of your parents?"

"I don't know. I can't help it, I'm just confused."

Ryan took her hands and gently kissed each one. "Your hands are cold."

"I know."

"Sukie, tell me what's wrong."

"I never told you about my ninth birthday."

"What about it?"

"My dad bought me a special present. It was a beautiful white dress, like a wedding gown. He and my mom made me model it for them. It fit perfectly on my straight, skinny body.

"You didn't like the dress? But you said it was beautiful."

"That's not the point. The next weekend, my parents made me put the gown on again. My dad wore his best tuxedo. My mom put a wreath of white flowers in my hair. My dad then took me to a special ceremony in our church. The pews were filled with other girls, all of us around nine or ten years old, and their daddies. Each couple took their turn to walk down the aisle up to a man dressed in white robes. There were candles in silver holders on tables behind the altar. Behind the candles were bouquets of white lilies."

"Sounds like a KKK meeting."

"No. It was a purity ball. At the altar, I was made to swear to my father that I would remain pure, a virgin until my wedding day. I didn't know exactly what a virgin was. Daddy took my hand and stared into my eyes as I repeated the solemn vow the man in white robes told me to say. After my dad swore to always protect my purity, he took a silver ring out of his pocket and put it on my finger. Then the so-called priest gave me a card with the words of my vow printed on it. My dad leaned down and whispered to me to always carry that card with me, and never forget my vow. Then, he kissed me lightly on the lips. I was now a purity ball bride."

"Sukie, this sounds to me like you grew up on another planet."

"I know. Maybe I did. But I didn't realize it at the time. They were my parents. Anyway, after all the couples had walked down the aisle and said their vows, the organ began to play. We went in a procession to the reception room next to the sanctuary, and the whole roomful of fathers and purity brides began to dance."

"Where's the ring now?"

"I threw it in the Seine the first night I was in Paris. I had outgrown it."

"Had you?"

"Hold me."

And Ryan held her tight. "Your whole body's cold," he murmured. Eventually, they fell asleep. Until Sukie's nightmare.

Early the next afternoon, Ryan sadly packed his suitcase. "You're sure you're okay, Sukie?"

"I'm fine. I knew this would happen someday, that they would show up out of the blue just to check on my lifestyle, just to make sure that their little angel is still lily white, still pure, unsullied by such grotesque things as men." Sukie nervously looked at her watch. "You need to go. They said five, but it's just like them to arrive hours early to try and catch me by surprise."

"Do I really have to leave you, Sukie?"

"Yes. You have to stay away! They can't see you. Don't even dream of coming back till after you see my parents leave."

Ryan kissed her gently. "I'll stay in the cafe until you come get me."

"Promise?"

"Promise."

"Alright. Thank you for understanding. Now hurry. Go! And don't worry, I'll be fine."

Ryan nodded, picked up his suitcase and left the flat. Slowly, he crossed the street to the Midi. In spite of his anger and frustration, he automatically scanned the room as he headed toward a window table. Of course, Green was in his normal seat praying to the gods of exotic pharmaceuticals. At the bar stood a small man with a pale face shriveled like a walnut. The man was delicately feeding bits of a *croque monsieur* to a white rat in a tiny cage set in front of him on the counter. Although he must have been past his mid-80s, the man's tight, blue T-shirt revealed surprisingly developed forearms and toned, bulging biceps. Popeye. And—but Ryan drew a blank on the rat. Oh, to hell with it, Ryan thought. The game had lost its savor without Sukie.

Ryan tried to envision Sukie politely, but firmly, telling her parents that she was now an adult, and that, although she loved them, she had to make her own choices. No longer a child, it was time for her to put away childish things. Her parents would have to accept the truth of what she said. This would free Sukie of the effects of her guilt-ridden childhood; it would liberate her to be with him, Ryan thought. Yes, if only her parents' hold on her could somehow be broken, one way or another.

Of course. It had to happen. Green materialized next to Ryan and fixed him with a beady stare. "Try humming E-flat for an hour," he rasped.

"Thank you, Green. Your advice is always appreciated."

Green vanished. And Ryan returned to his melancholy musings. What are they going to do to her? They're not going to beat her. No, not physically. But they will humiliate her, reduce her to tears. Did she secretly want me to stay with her, protect her? Did I leave her just because I lack the balls to stand up to some fat-assed, fundamentalist proctologist and his scrawny, uptight wife?

Ryan bitterly delighted in imagining that the shape of the good doctor's head—pointed at the top and broader at the cheeks—was a plus for a doctor in Wittmore's chosen field. After all, there would be occasions during a colonoscopy when the miniature video camera failed, and Wittmore would be required to launch an on-site investigation with the naked eye.

Maybe I should storm across the street, intercept them, tell them that she's with me now and they can go fuck themselves. Yeah, I like that idea. But how would Sukie react to that? Would she hate me for interfering? So here I sit in a secure state of inertia, arguing with myself, a refried Hamlet.

Ryan sipped his coffee, and then abruptly set the cup back on the table. There they were, unmistakable. One bloated Botero sculpture waddling up the Boulevard Raspail, arm-in-arm with a pencil-thin Giacometti. Ryan wanted to leap up, run across the street, and stop them. But something held him back. Am I afraid? he wondered. No. She has to confront them someday. And she has to do it on her own. So be it.

Dr. Wittmore pushed the button for Sukie's flat. In a moment, she answered on the intercom. "Who's there?"

"It's your parents, Susanna Katherine," said her father.

Sukie pushed the buzzer and the street door clicked open. In a few moments, her father knocked at her door.

"Hi, it's so good to see you," Sukie said brightly, with her high-school-picture smile.

"Guess you get your exercise living here," said the doctor, slightly out of breath.

"Oh yeah, the stairs. You get used to them."

Nobody made a move to hug, or even to shake hands. "I think it's a lovely little place," said her mother, "from what I can see out here in the hallway."

"Well, come in, come in," Sukie beamed. "You must be tired after your long trip," she said, and she gestured them inside. Her father, a very observant man, glanced casually around the flat.

"Yes, it is a cozy place," he declared. "Just the right size so you don't feel lonely living by yourself, right Susanna?"

"Absolutely," Sukie agreed.

"Well, I think it's charming," her mother reiterated. "So delightfully rustic."

Sukie motioned toward the small leather couch. "Please, sit down." They sat. Her mother—tall and long-waisted—now appeared to be a full head taller than Dr. Wittmore, whose body formed a smoothly flowing triangle from the apex of his crown down to his size 45 belt.

Sukie dragged a wooden chair from the table and sat across the room from her parents. "Can I make you some coffee, or something?"

"No thanks, Susanna," said her dad.

"Oh no, don't go to any trouble for us, my dear," her mother added.

Dr. Wittmore leaned toward Sukie and endeavored unsuccessfully to put a twinkle in his eye. "So how are the French treating you, Susanna Katherine?"

"Very well. I love my students, and the families are very kind."

"That's great, Susanna," he said. "I'm sure the kids will all be sorry to see you leave."

Her mother nodded in agreement. "But everyone at the church will be very happy to welcome you back." She pursed her lips in what might have been a smile.

Dr. Wittmore glanced meaningfully at his wife. "They sure will, particularly some of the young men."

"Oh yes, Susanna. That nice Peter Watley keeps asking about you every Sunday."

"He's become quite a handsome young man, don't you think so, Ardyss?"

"Oh yes. It's amazing how much a person can change in the space of less than a year."

"That's very true, Mother. Perhaps I can make you some tea? I'm sorry I don't have any cookies. It's just that ... your visit was so unexpected."

"Well, we thought we'd surprise you, Susanna, didn't we Ardyss?"

"Oh yes. We knew you'd be happy to see some familiar faces."

"So, what do you do for entertainment after your classes? You must have made some girlfriends by now."

"A few, Father, mostly American college students."

Her father nodded approval. "Good. Where do you and your friends go?"

"To the movies, mostly. Sometimes the theater, or a cafe for coffee."

"Not out to restaurants?" her mother asked.

"No, not often. Restaurants are too expensive."

Her parents exchanged a glance. "Well, we thought we'd take you out to a nice place for dinner tonight," her mother declared.

"Absolutely. Give our daughter a real night on the town," her father boomed. "But first, where's your restroom, Susanna? I need to wash my hands."

"It's right through the kitchen, Dad. There's a fresh bar of soap on the bathroom sink and a clean towel on the rack next to it."

The doctor stood. "I'll be just a moment."

As her father left for the bathroom, her mother got up and walked over to the bookshelf. Sukie got up and paced, and then went over to the window. She looked across the street to where Ryan was faithfully waiting.

"My, my. So many books, so many writers." Mrs. Wittmore pulled a paperback off the shelf. "What's this? *Tropic of Cancer* by Henry Miller. Never heard of it. What's it about?"

"Just a book about Paris, Mom. No, you wouldn't know it."

Her mother pulled out another book. "What's this one about? *Tales of a Victorian Housemaid*. I never knew you were so interested in history, Susanna. You're not in college anymore."

Sukie turned away from the window. "Oh, that book's kind of like a Charles Dickens story." She was relieved when her mother put the books back on the shelf.

Sukie began to worry about her father. The longer he was absent, the more nervous she became. What's he doing? Sukie wondered. Although she'd carefully sanitized the apartment for their arrival, she didn't like her father to be out of her sight. Had she forgotten something?

Abruptly, Dr. Wittmore came out of the bathroom and planted himself next to his wife, hands clasped behind his back. He stared coldly at Sukie. "So, Susanna Katherine, once again, what do you do for entertainment in the evenings?"

A sense of dread slowly settled in Sukie's body. Something was wrong. It was clear from her father's expression. "I already told you. The movies. Or sometimes the theater, or even just read a book."

"And you do this alone? Or perhaps with a girlfriend?"

This was getting surreal. What right did he have to interrogate her about who she went to the movies with? Sukie started to tremble. Her mother, at first confused, now caught her father's drift, and turned a stern glance upon her daughter.

"I asked you a question, Susanna Katherine," her father barked.

Sukie's shaking increased. "Yes, sometimes with a friend."

"A *girl*friend?"

"Yes." He has no right, thought Sukie. He can't pick my clothes anymore, and he can't pick my friends.

"Do your *girl*friends ever spend the night?"

"What do you mean?" Sukie's hearing began to dim. Her whole face felt hot.

"Susanna Katherine, you know exactly what I mean! Don't you lie to me, young lady. That's a sin."

Sukie tried to speak but no sound came out.

"Answer me!" her father thundered. Suddenly, he whipped his hands out from behind his back and waved a pair of Ryan's underwear in Sukie's face. "Tell me what girlfriend would wear these!"

The clothes hamper, Sukie realized. He picked through my dirty laundry!

"Or have you taken to wearing men's undergarments with a 32-inch waist," he sneered.

Sukie was astonished. Oh my God, he's even read the label!

"Are you living in sin?" gasped her mother.

Her father glowered. "Aren't you saving yourself for marriage? Have you forgotten your vow? And where's the ring I gave you?"

For a moment, Sukie stared in horror at her father. Then she gave a piercing shriek, and ran into the bedroom. She emerged with her carefully hidden shoebox. Her shaking had stopped. "You missed something, father dear," she said calmly. Susanna Katherine had found her voice. "Your search wasn't thorough enough." And she emptied her entire array of novelty items onto the kitchen counter.

Time to confront the Devil. Her own private Devil from her own private nightmares now stood before her, exultant, triumphant, brandishing with satanic pride the underwear of Ryan Aedan.

Sukie grabbed a tube of personal lubricant and waved it in front of her father. "Do you know what this is?" she hissed. "You, Dr. Wittmore, of all people, should know some of its uses." She grabbed a butt plug. "Do you know what my boyfriends do with this, Daddy?" She picked up a dildo and waved it in her mother's face. "Ever seen one of these, Mommy?" Her mother, to her credit, did recognize the shape, but had never imagined that it might be the subject of a rubber replica. Sukie emptied a box of condoms onto the floor. "Surely you've seen those before," she cooed. "After all, I am an only child."

Her parents stood motionless and mute. Two pillars of salt.

Sukie was through being afraid and made to feel ashamed of being a woman. Never again would mommy and daddy censor her clothes. Never again would their faces monitor her bedroom. Never again would their ghosts invade her dreams with suspicion and disapproval. Sukie continued to goad them as she grabbed various other items. "What's this? And this? And this?"

Abruptly, Sukie stopped. She had achieved the ninth circle of her outrage: ice. She narrowed her eyes, and slowly smiled. Sukie reached back and picked up a long, flesh-colored vibrator. She cradled it tenderly in both hands and slowly raised it to her lips. Her delicate pink tongue quietly peeped forth, and then glided serpent-like around the tip. She continued to glare at her parents as her tongue began to slowly explore the shaft.

The tableau was finally broken by Dr. Wittmore. "Jezebel. Jezebel. The Devil has seized you, Susanna Katherine." Dr. Wittmore took his stunned wife's arm. "Come, dear," he muttered. "We have lost our daughter to iniquity and Hell fire." And, none too gently, he ushered his wife from the apartment.

Sukie stared at the closed door for a moment, and then looked around the room. Her novelty items—at least the unbreakable ones—lay scattered across the hardwood floor. She took the shoebox and mechanically picked them up, took the others from the counter, went into her bedroom, and placed the toys back in the drawer where they belonged. She threw the empty shoebox into her tiny closet, came out through the bathroom, sat on the couch, and cried.

A few moments later, Ryan softly opened the apartment door. "Sukie. Why are you crying?" He sat on the couch next to her, and put his arm around her. "I saw them leaving. They looked angry. What's going on?" Sukie didn't respond. "I waited till they were out of sight, then I had to come back. I couldn't just sit there wondering how you were. Please talk to me."

"My father doesn't love me anymore."

"Sukie, I'm sure that's not true, whatever he might have said."

"Ryan, you have to go back to your hotel."

"Why? Are they coming back? What happened?"

"Let's go for a walk."

Ryan's memory of the evening was a jumbled collage of images, jagged shards of a bad dream morphing into one another. He couldn't make any sense out of what Sukie had told him. Which wasn't much. Only that she might never see her parents again. That she had broken something between herself and them—especially her father—that could never be fixed. Nothing could be that bad, Ryan had told her. Sukie hadn't responded. Ryan had waited for her to say something, anything. "Please, tell me what happened," he'd said over and over. All she would say was that her father didn't love her anymore. They had walked side by side, not touching. At the river, they'd automatically turned toward St. Michel, not speaking, till Sukie would mutter something like "and so they left me," and would fail to answer Ryan's pleading for an explanation. They'd drifted on, apart. Quai Voltaire, Quai Malaquais, Quai de Conti, Quai des Grands Augustins. Crowds of pedestrians flowed around them and the screaming traffic streamed by. Finally, Place St. Michel. Ryan had persuaded her to sit down at an outside table. "You must be hungry," he'd said. Why did that sound so stupid? "I'm sorry," she'd said. "It's not your fault." Ryan knew one probable reason for her upset, but why was he afraid to mention it? The thing about her ring, her vow. He knew that had to be part of the problem. But wait a minute, he'd told himself. He wasn't the one who had first helped her break it. And that thought made him jealous and angry. And then he'd been angry at himself for feeling that way, because that feeling was unworthy and unwarranted when Sukie clearly needed his help, someone's help, and it should be his, and he couldn't seem to find the way, any way, to help her. Still more walking, through crowds of couples on narrow sidewalks, tiny streets, parked cars jammed bumper to bumper, cafes and restaurants overflowing with couples, laughing, eating, drinking, talking, touching, till once again it was after midnight. Rue Brea was dark and quiet. "Please, sleep on the couch tonight," she'd said, "And in the morning, please go back to your hotel, your suitcase is still packed." That sounded so cold—your hotel … suitcase still packed … and what had he done to make Sukie say that? "For how long?" he'd managed to ask. "I don't know, just for a time." "I don't want to leave you," he'd said. "You must," she'd said, "just for a time, please."

And so at dawn, as the buses again began to wheeze and roar up and down Boulevard Raspail, Ryan had taken his suitcase down the stairs and out to the sidewalk. He'd slowly walked up to Boulevard du Montparnasse, and then headed toward the train station in search of a cafe that was open early.

As his solitary days and nights wore on, Ryan spent most of his free time walking aimlessly about the city. But everywhere he went, he remembered prior walks with Sukie. Every glass of wine, every cafe au lait, every croissant, everything reminded him of Sukie. And he cursed his memory games.

Ryan had long been an avid student of historical irony. It fascinated him to see how often the greatest efforts of people who'd had the best intentions could result in the opposite of what they had hoped for and worked to achieve. Now he was a victim of such irony. The smashing of the bonds with her parents, rather than freeing her, had made Sukie unable to be with him.

Ryan's friend at the restaurant was sympathetic, and

sometimes let him work longer hours to fill the void. Once, Ryan went out for a glass of wine with an attractive co-worker. She invited him to dinner back in her apartment. Ryan declined. What was wrong with him? he asked himself. Before he met Sukie, he would have accepted the invitation with great pleasure.

And now? What was Sukie doing? It wasn't fair. Why was *he* so lonely and yet trapped, bound by memories, unable to happily keep seeking the distant palace of wisdom? Logically, he should now be free. Besides, he had always been faintly disappointed, sometimes even annoyed, that he had encountered Sukie so soon. He'd anticipated the need for a far more exhaustive search. However, no argument, no enticement, nothing worked to free him.

The second month of Ryan's exile began. In the first month, he'd sat in the Café du Midi every evening, waiting, hoping that Sukie would come to him. Twice, he'd called her, and twice, she'd asked him to give her more time. On the third call, he'd gotten angry. "Sukie, what are you doing? I'm not going to wait around forever. This isn't fair." And he'd hung up.

A week later, he stopped going to the Midi. She knows where my hotel is, he thought. Serve her right if I just moved out and never saw her again. But he stayed.

What *was* Sukie doing? Even Sukie didn't really know. She was free. She should have rejoiced in her liberty. But she felt only emptiness. As the lonely weeks dragged on, she continued to tutor her students, then walk back to her empty apartment and sit alone on the couch. In the late afternoon, she would stand at the window, looking across the street, waiting for Ryan to show up at the Midi. Why couldn't she just walk over and meet him?

She knew that her loneliness had nothing to do with her parents' church. She had stopped believing in any formal religion a long time ago. But her parents? They were gone. And she began to realize just how much they had been her anchor and her life raft. In their absence, she had nothing and no one to rebel against. Dimly, Sukie began to understand that she truly was responsible for her own choices. She had to accept that responsibility. She didn't have to justify her decisions to anyone else. Only to herself.

Sukie felt she was living in a vacuum. She even began to have doubts about her relationship with Ryan. Did she live with him simply to defy her parents? Certainly, her relationship with Ryan was a direct challenge to her father. Now, in the void, what did she feel? Was she ready to love Ryan? To love anyone? How much experience had she had? Did she know enough? But in spite of all Sukie's doubts, as each day passed, she missed Ryan more.

Then, one day, Ryan was gone. He wasn't at the Midi. She waited at the window for hours. Where was he? Who was he with? Tomorrow, she assured herself, he'll be there. But he wasn't. Nor the following day. Nor the following. What's happened? Has he left me? Ryan's image began to occupy Sukie's every waking thought. She started to realize just how much she wanted him. I can't lose him, she told herself. I can't let him go. On the morning of the fifth day, Sukie wrote a note, and carried it over to Ryan's hotel. She was greatly relieved to learn that he was still registered.

When Ryan returned from work, the receptionist smiled and handed him the envelope. "*C'est pour vous, monsieur.*" Ryan put it in his jacket pocket, and climbed the stairs to his room.

Now what? he wondered. Does she think I'll just come running back to her? That I'm her servant, her puppet? Or is this going to be her way of saying goodbye? Or, maybe she'll say she wants more time. More time. For what? Ryan knew that anger is often an effective bulwark against disappointment. He had occasionally used that ploy on himself. But this time was different.

Ryan left the hotel with the unopened envelope still in his jacket pocket and walked toward Boulevard du Montparnasse. At the corner, he wavered. What now? Perhaps a glass of red at the Select to start the evening early? I'll read the note tomorrow. Or I could go across the river to observe the automotive gladiatorial combat around the Arc de Triomphe. Maybe throw the envelope in the river on the way. And change hotels in the morning. Then again, there's always the chance that my waitress friend isn't busy tonight. Perhaps a phone call is in order. He stared at the statue of Balzac. It smiled at him. Lighten up, Ryan. You are naught but a microbe in the human comedy. Ryan looked across at Rue Brea. He glanced back at the statue. And then, with a sense of doom, Ryan crossed Raspail and walked down to the Café du Midi.

He entered, automatically scanned the room and registered nothing except that Green was there, immersed in his mental prayer wheel. Ryan sat down, took the envelope from his pocket, and carefully placed it on the table. Suddenly, Green was at Ryan's side. Oh no. Not now, Green. Green stared at him for a moment, slowly smiled, then shuffled with great dignity back to his own table.

Ryan stared at the envelope. Admit it, Ryan. You're afraid to open it. He picked it up—felt a presence—and there stood Sukie. Now what? Has she summoned the nerve to bid me farewell in person? Ryan looked at her, and then slowly opened the envelope. He pulled out the note: *Could we have dinner tonight? I promise to tell you a funny story.* He looked up at Sukie.

"I love you, Ryan."

Ryan took a deep breath, exhaled slowly, carefully put the note back in the envelope, and put it in his pocket. He closed his eyes, leaned back in his chair, and laced his hands behind his head. When he finally opened his eyes, Sukie hadn't moved. "So," he said. "What's the funny story?"

ACKNOWLEDGMENTS

Initial thanks to Inbae Bhang for—once upon a time—asking me a question. Also, many thanks to Joanne Williams, Linda Xiques, Jill Kramer and Liz Stewart for their advice and support as I began to explore these stories. Particular thanks to Patty Marra for her incisive comments, and to Phil Chomak for his careful reading and lucid critiques. Very special thanks to Sharon Lightholder for her generosity of spirit, keen editorial eye and constant encouragement. My heartfelt thanks go to Renee Humphrey for her insightful commentary. Also thanks to Eliza Frye for her sensitive illustrations and cover design, and to Jim Shubin for his book design expertise. And finally, most of all, thanks to Terry —for everything.

ABOUT THE AUTHOR

After graduating with a degree in English from Stanford, Jay Humphrey pursued a varied career in theater and television, law, writing and teaching. *The Day You Love Me* is his first collection of short stories. This book is fiction, but as Albert Camus noted, fiction is the lie through which we tell the truth. Jay lives with his wife in Northern California.

jaylewishumphrey.com

www.ingramcontent.com/pod-product-compliance
Lightning Source LLC
Chambersburg PA
CBHW020609300426
44113CB00007B/566